# BIBLE'S PROMISES

# FOR WOMEN

### ENGLISH STANDARD VERSION

CROSSWAY BIBLES

A DIVISION OF
GOOD NEWS PUBLISHERS
WHEATON, ILLINOIS

| DP | | 13 | 12 | 11 | 10 | 09 | 08 | 07 | 06 | 05 | 04 | 03 |
|----|----|----|----|----|----|----|----|----|----|----|----|----|
| 15 | 14 | 13 | 12 | 11 | 10 | 9 | 8 | 7 | 6 | 5 | 4 | 3 | 2 | 1 |

# TABLE OF CONTENTS

# FOREWORD

We live in an age when countless voices shout con-
flicting messages about what's true. But human spec-
ulation and worldly wisdom hold no real security
for a woman looking for truth upon which to build
her life.

God's Word gives us truth we can trust. The promises we find there come from the One who made us
to be his daughters and loved us enough to send his
Son to die for our sins. The Bible provides trustworthy guidance and sure hope for every woman who
seeks to live a redeemed life of beauty and holiness.

*The Bible's Promises for Women* consists entirely of
selections from Scripture, arranged by topic, to help
you build a spiritual foundation for your life. These
passages are all taken from the *Holy Bible: English
Standard Version*, a translation of the Bible known
for its word-for-word accuracy, clarity, beauty, and
readability.

Our prayer is that the truth found in these verses
will encourage you and lead you to draw close to your
Heavenly Father through his Son, Jesus.

*The Publishers*

# Acceptance

Welcome one another as Christ has welcomed you, for the glory of God.

ROMANS 15:7

"And the King will answer them, 'Truly, I say to you, as you did it to one of the least of these my brothers, you did it to me.'"

MATTHEW 25:40

As for the one who is weak in faith, welcome him, but not to quarrel over opinions.

ROMANS 14:1

I commend to you our sister Phoebe, a servant of the church at Cenchreae, that you may welcome her in the Lord in a way worthy of the saints, and help her in whatever she may need from you, for she has been a patron of many and of myself as well.

ROMANS 16:1-2

Beloved, let us love one another, for love is from God, and whoever loves has been born of God and knows God.

1 JOHN 4:7

# ADOPTION

[Jesus said,] "I will not leave you as orphans; I will come to you."

JOHN 14:18

When the child grew up, she brought him to Pharaoh's daughter, and he became her son. She named him Moses, "Because," she said, "I drew him out of the water."

EXODUS 2:10

He was bringing up Hadassah, that is Esther, the daughter of his uncle, for she had neither father nor mother. The young woman had a beautiful figure and was lovely to look at, and when her father and her mother died, Mordecai took her as his own daughter.

ESTHER 2:7

When Israel was a child, I loved him,
   and out of Egypt I called my son.

HOSEA 11:1

For you did not receive the spirit of slavery to fall back into fear, but you have received the Spirit of adoption as sons, by whom we cry, "Abba! Father!" The Spirit himself bears witness with our spirit that we are children of God.

ROMANS 8:15-16

# BEAUTY

Charm is deceitful, and beauty is vain,
    but a woman who fears the LORD is to be praised.

PROVERBS 31:30

Let your adorning be the hidden person of the heart
with the imperishable beauty of a gentle and quiet
spirit.

1 PETER 3:4

How beautiful upon the mountains
    are the feet of him who brings good news,
who publishes peace, who brings good news of
        happiness,
    who publishes salvation,
    who says to Zion, "Your God reigns."

ISAIAH 52:7

One thing have I asked of the LORD,
    that will I seek after:
that I may dwell in the house of the LORD
    all the days of my life,
to gaze upon the beauty of the LORD
    and to inquire in his temple.

PSALM 27:4

# Calling of God

You . . . are called to belong to Jesus Christ.

ROMANS 1:6

But you are a chosen race, a royal priesthood, a holy nation, a people for his own possession, that you may proclaim the excellencies of him who called you out of darkness into his marvelous light.

1 PETER 2:9

But we ought always to give thanks to God for you, brothers beloved by the Lord, because God chose you as the firstfruits to be saved, through sanctification by the Spirit and belief in the truth. To this he called you through our gospel, so that you may obtain the glory of our Lord Jesus Christ.

2 THESSALONIANS 2:13-14

And we know that for those who love God all things work together for good, for those who are called according to his purpose.

ROMANS 8:28

For you were called to freedom, brothers. Only do not use your freedom as an opportunity for the flesh, but through love serve one another.

GALATIANS 5:13

I press on toward the goal for the prize of the upward call of God in Christ Jesus.

PHILIPPIANS 3:14

God is faithful, by whom you were called into the fellowship of his Son, Jesus Christ our Lord.

1 CORINTHIANS 1:9

For God has not called us for impurity, but in holiness.

1 THESSALONIANS 4:7

Fight the good fight of the faith. Take hold of the eternal life to which you were called and about which you made the good confession in the presence of many witnesses.

1 TIMOTHY 6:12

# CHEER

When the cares of my heart are many,
    your consolations cheer my soul.

PSALM 94:19

Is anyone cheerful? Let him sing praise.

JAMES 5:13

I will greatly rejoice in the LORD;
    my soul shall exult in my God,
for he has clothed me with the garments of
        salvation;
    he has covered me with the robe of
        righteousness,
as a bridegroom decks himself like a priest with a
        beautiful headdress,
    and as a bride adorns herself with her jewels.

ISAIAH 61:10

[Jesus said,] "These things I have spoken to you, that my joy may be in you, and that your joy may be full."

JOHN 15:11

# CHILDREN

[Jesus said,] "Whoever receives one such child in my name receives me, but whoever causes one of these little ones who believe in me to sin, it would be better for him to have a great millstone fastened around his neck and to be drowned in the depth of the sea."

MATTHEW 18:5 6

A wise son makes a glad father,
but a foolish son is a sorrow to his mother.

PROVERBS 10:1

[Jesus said,] "Truly, I say to you, whoever does not receive the kingdom of God like a child shall not enter it."

MARK 10:15

At that time Jesus declared, "I thank you, Father, Lord of heaven and earth, that you have hidden these things from the wise and understanding and revealed them to little children."

MATTHEW 11:25

# CLEANSING

Wash me thoroughly from my iniquity,
and cleanse me from my sin! . . .
Purge me with hyssop, and I shall be clean;
wash me, and I shall be whiter than snow.

PSALM 51:2, 7

Since we have these promises, beloved, let us cleanse
ourselves from every defilement of body and spirit,
bringing holiness to completion in the fear of God.

2 CORINTHIANS 7:1

Come now, let us reason together, says the LORD:
though your sins are like scarlet,
they shall be as white as snow;
though they are red like crimson,
they shall become like wool.

ISAIAH 1:18

Peter said to him, "You shall never wash my feet."
Jesus answered him, "If I do not wash you, you have
no share with me."

JOHN 13:8

If we confess our sins, he is faithful and just to forgive
us our sins and to cleanse us from all unrighteousness.

1 JOHN 1:9

# CLOTHING

Rend your hearts and not your garments.
    Return to the LORD, your God,
for he is gracious and merciful,
    slow to anger, and abounding in steadfast love;
and he relents over disaster.

JOEL 2:13

Do not let your adorning be external—the braiding of hair, the wearing of gold, or the putting on of clothing.

1 PETER 3:3

Show no partiality as you hold the faith in our Lord Jesus Christ, the Lord of glory. For if a man wearing a gold ring and fine clothing comes into your assembly, and a poor man in shabby clothing also comes in, and if you pay attention to the one who wears the fine clothing and say, "You sit here in a good place," while you say to the poor man, "You stand over there," or, "Sit down at my feet," have you not then made distinctions among yourselves and become judges with evil thoughts?

JAMES 2:1-4

# COMMUNITY

For as in one body we have many members, and the members do not all have the same function, so we, though many, are one body in Christ, and individually members one of another.

ROMANS 12:4-5

And all who believed were together and had all things in common.

ACTS 2:44

And let us consider how to stir up one another to love and good works, not neglecting to meet together, as is the habit of some, but encouraging one another, and all the more as you see the Day drawing near.

HEBREWS 10:24-25

For in one Spirit we were all baptized into one body—Jews or Greeks, slaves or free—and all were made to drink of one Spirit.

1 CORINTHIANS 12:13

Rejoice with those who rejoice, weep with those who weep.

ROMANS 12:15

# CONFIDENCE

The LORD will be your confidence.

PROVERBS 3:26

For I am sure that neither death nor life, nor angels nor rulers, nor things present nor things to come, nor powers, nor height nor depth, nor anything else in all creation, will be able to separate us from the love of God in Christ Jesus our Lord.

ROMANS 8:38-39

For you, O Lord, are my hope,
    my trust, O LORD, from my youth.

PSALM 71:5

And this is the confidence that we have toward him, that if we ask anything according to his will he hears us. And if we know that he hears us in whatever we ask, we know that we have the requests that we have asked of him.

1 JOHN 5:14-15

Have I not commanded you? Be strong and courageous. Do not be frightened, and do not be dismayed, for the LORD your God is with you wherever you go."

JOSHUA 1:9

# CONTENTMENT

[Jesus said,] "Therefore I tell you, do not be anxious about your life, what you will eat or what you will drink, nor about your body, what you will put on. Is not life more than food, and the body more than clothing?"

MATTHEW 6:25

Keep your life free from love of money, and be content with what you have, for he has said, "I will never leave you nor forsake you."

HEBREWS 13:5

I have learned in whatever situation I am to be content. I know how to be brought low, and I know how to abound. In any and every circumstance, I have learned the secret of facing plenty and hunger, abundance and need. I can do all things through him who strengthens me.

PHILIPPIANS 4:11-13

Now there is great gain in godliness with contentment, for we brought nothing into the world, and we cannot take anything out of the world. But if we have food and clothing, with these we will be content.

1 TIMOTHY 6:6-8

# CONVICTION OF THE HEART

Fight the good fight of the faith. Take hold of the eternal life to which you were called and about which you made the good confession in the presence of many witnesses.

1 TIMOTHY 6:12

For we know, brothers loved by God, that he has chosen you, because our gospel came to you not only in word, but also in power and in the Holy Spirit and with full conviction. You know what kind of men we proved to be among you for your sake.

1 THESSALONIANS 1:4-5

Now faith is the assurance of things hoped for, the conviction of things not seen.

HEBREWS 11:1

Let us draw near with a true heart in full assurance of faith, with our hearts sprinkled clean from an evil conscience and our bodies washed with pure water.

HEBREWS 10:22

So we do not lose heart. Though our outer nature is wasting away, our inner nature is being renewed day by day.

2 CORINTHIANS 4:16

By this we shall know that we are of the truth and reassure our heart before him; for whenever our heart condemns us, God is greater than our heart, and he knows everything. Beloved, if our heart does not condemn us, we have confidence before God.

1 JOHN 3:19-21

For I want you to know how great a struggle I have for you and for those at Laodicea and for all who have not seen me face to face, that their hearts may be encouraged, being knit together in love, to reach all the riches of full assurance of understanding and the knowledge of God's mystery, which is Christ.

COLOSSIANS 2:1-2

For we know, brothers loved by God, that he has chosen you.

1 THESSALONIANS 1:4

For I know that my Redeemer lives,
    and at the last he will stand upon the earth.

JOB 19:25

For I am sure that neither death nor life, nor angels nor rulers, nor things present nor things to come, nor powers, nor height nor depth, nor anything else in all creation, will be able to separate us from the love of God in Christ Jesus our Lord.

ROMANS 8:38-39

# COVENANT

But this is the covenant that I will make with the house of Israel after those days, declares the LORD: I will put my law within them, and I will write it on their hearts. And I will be their God, and they shall be my people.

JEREMIAH 31:33

But to all who did receive [Jesus], who believed in his name, he gave the right to become children of God.

JOHN 1:12

But when the fullness of time had come, God sent forth his Son, born of woman, born under the law, to redeem those who were under the law, so that we might receive adoption as sons.

GALATIANS 4:4-5

Know therefore that the LORD your God is God, the faithful God who keeps covenant and steadfast love with those who love him and keep his command-ments, to a thousand generations.

DEUTERONOMY 7:9

# CREATION

In the beginning, God created the heavens and the earth. The earth was without form and void, and darkness was over the face of the deep. And the Spirit of God was hovering over the face of the waters.

GENESIS 1:1-2

For by him all things were created, in heaven and on earth, visible and invisible, whether thrones or dominions or rulers or authorities—all things were created through him and for him. And he is before all things, and in him all things hold together.

COLOSSIANS 1:16-17

So God created man in his own image,
    in the image of God he created him;
    male and female he created them.

GENESIS 1:27

So the LORD God caused a deep sleep to fall upon the man, and while he slept took one of his ribs and closed up its place with flesh. And the rib that the LORD God had taken from the man he made into a woman and brought her to the man.

GENESIS 2:21-22

# DEDICATION

But Hannah did not go up, for she said to her husband, "As soon as the child is weaned, I will bring him, so that he may appear in the presence of the LORD and dwell there forever."

1 SAMUEL 1:22

The sacrifices of God are a broken spirit;
a broken and contrite heart, O God, you will not despise.

PSALM 51:17

I appeal to you therefore, brothers, by the mercies of God, to present your bodies as a living sacrifice, holy and acceptable to God, which is your spiritual worship.

ROMANS 12:1

My son, give me your heart,
and let your eyes observe my ways.

PROVERBS 23:26

But no devoted thing that a man devotes to the LORD, of anything that he has, whether man or beast, or of his inherited field, shall be sold or redeemed; every devoted thing is most holy to the LORD.

LEVITICUS 27:28

# DELIGHT

Delight yourself in the LORD,
    and he will give you the desires of your heart.

PSALM 37:4

As an apple tree among the trees of the forest,
    so is my beloved among the young men.
With great delight I sat in his shadow,
    and his fruit was sweet to my taste.

SONG 2:3

"Delight yourself in the Almighty
    and lift up your face to God.
You will make your prayer to him, and he will hear
        you."

JOB 22:26-27

Praise the LORD! Blessed is the man who fears the
        LORD,
    who greatly delights in his commandments!

PSALM 112:1

Let your mercy come to me, that I may live;
    for your law is my delight.

PSALM 119:77

# Desires

Delight yourself in the LORD,
>and he will give you the desires of your heart.

PSALM 37:4

As a deer pants for flowing streams,
>so pants my soul for you, O God.
My soul thirsts for God,
>for the living God.

PSALM 42:1-2

Whom have I in heaven but you?
>And there is nothing on earth that I desire
>>besides you.

PSALM 73:25

You will seek me and find me. When you seek me
with all your heart, I will be found by you, declares
the LORD.

JEREMIAH 29:13-14

"Blessed are those who hunger and thirst for righteousness, for they shall be satisfied."

MATTHEW 5:6

# DEVOTION

I appeal to you therefore, brothers, by the mercies of God, to present your bodies as a living sacrifice, holy and acceptable to God, which is your spiritual worship.

ROMANS 12:1

Fear the LORD and serve him faithfully with all your heart. For consider what great things he has done for you.

1 SAMUEL 12:24

Walk in a manner worthy of God, who calls you into his own kingdom and glory.

1 THESSALONIANS 2:12

Do you not know that your body is a temple of the Holy Spirit within you, whom you have from God? You are not your own, for you were bought with a price. So glorify God in your body.

1 CORINTHIANS 6:19-20

Honor the LORD with your wealth
   and with the firstfruits of all your produce.

PROVERBS 3:9

So therefore, any one of you who does not renounce all that he has cannot be my disciple.

LUKE 14:33

# DILIGENCE

Now set your mind and heart to seek the LORD your God.

1 CHRONICLES 22:19

You shall diligently keep the commandments of the LORD your God, and his testimonies and his statutes, which he has commanded you.

DEUTERONOMY 6:17

And if you will indeed obey my commandments that I command you today, to love the LORD your God, and to serve him with all your heart and with all your soul, he will give the rain for your land in its season, the early rain and the later rain, that you may gather in your grain and your wine and your oil.

DEUTERONOMY 11:13-14

Keep your heart with all vigilance,
    for from it flow the springs of life.

PROVERBS 4:23

Therefore, brothers, be all the more diligent to make your calling and election sure, for if you practice these qualities you will never fall.

2 PETER 1:10

Whatever your hand finds to do, do it with your might, for there is no work or thought or knowledge or wisdom in Sheol, to which you are going.

ECCLESIASTES 9:10

But as you excel in everything—in faith, in speech, in knowledge, in all earnestness, and in our love for you—see that you excel in this act of grace also.

2 CORINTHIANS 8:7

Whoever diligently seeks good seeks favor,
    but evil comes to him who searches for it.

PROVERBS 11:27

And let us not grow weary of doing good, for in due season we will reap, if we do not give up.

GALATIANS 6:9

Therefore, my beloved brothers, be steadfast, immovable, always abounding in the work of the Lord, knowing that in the Lord your labor is not in vain.

1 CORINTHIANS 15:58

The hand of the diligent will rule,
    while the slothful will be put to forced labor.

PROVERBS 12:24

# DISCIPLINE

My son, do not despise the LORD's discipline
   or be weary of his reproof.

PROVERBS 3:11

It is for discipline that you have to endure. God is
treating you as sons. For what son is there whom his
father does not discipline?

HEBREWS 12:7

For the moment all discipline seems painful rather
than pleasant, but later it yields the peaceful fruit of
righteousness to those who have been trained by it.

HEBREWS 12:11

But when we are judged by the Lord, we are disci-
plined so that we may not be condemned along with
the world.

1 CORINTHIANS 11:32

As for those who persist in sin, rebuke them in the
presence of all, so that the rest may stand in fear.

1 TIMOTHY 5:20

Be ready in season and out of season; reprove, rebuke,
and exhort, with complete patience and teaching.

2 TIMOTHY 4:2

# DIVORCE

And Pharisees came up to him and tested him by asking, "Is it lawful to divorce one's wife for any cause?" He answered, "Have you not read that he who created them from the beginning made them male and female, and said, 'Therefore a man shall leave his father and his mother and hold fast to his wife, and they shall become one flesh'? So they are no longer two but one flesh. What therefore God has joined together, let not man separate." They said to him, "Why then did Moses command one to give a certificate of divorce and to send her away?" He said to them, "Because of your hardness of heart Moses allowed you to divorce your wives, but from the beginning it was not so. And I say to you: whoever divorces his wife, except for sexual immorality, and marries another, commits adultery."

MATTHEW 19:3-9

[Jesus said,] "It was also said, 'Whoever divorces his wife, let him give her a certificate of divorce.' But I say to you that everyone who divorces his wife, except on the ground of sexual immorality, makes her commit adultery. And whoever marries a divorced woman commits adultery."

MATTHEW 5:31-32

# ELECTION

[Jesus said,] "You did not choose me, but I chose you and appointed you that you should go and bear fruit and that your fruit should abide, so that whatever you ask the Father in my name, he may give it to you."

JOHN 15:16

[Jesus said,] "I have manifested your [the Father's] name to the people whom you gave me out of the world. Yours they were, and you gave them to me, and they have kept your word."

JOHN 17:6

[God] chose us in him before the foundation of the world, that we should be holy and blameless before him.

EPHESIANS 1:4

For we are [God's] workmanship, created in Christ Jesus for good works, which God prepared beforehand, that we should walk in them.

EPHESIANS 2:10

In [Christ] we have obtained an inheritance, having been predestined according to the purpose of him who works all things according to the counsel of his will.

EPHESIANS 1:11

# EMPOWERMENT

But [the Lord] said to me, "My grace is sufficient for you, for my power is made perfect in weakness." Therefore I will boast all the more gladly of my weaknesses, so that the power of Christ may rest upon me.

2 CORINTHIANS 12:9

He gives power to the faint,
    and to him who has no might he increases
        strength.
Even youths shall faint and be weary,
    and young men shall fall exhausted;
but they who wait for the LORD shall renew their
        strength;
    they shall mount up with wings like eagles;
they shall run and not be weary;
    they shall walk and not faint.

ISAIAH 40:29-31

[Jesus said,] "And these signs will accompany those who believe: in my name they will cast out demons; they will speak in new tongues; they will pick up serpents with their hands; and if they drink any deadly poison, it will not hurt them; they will lay their hands on the sick, and they will recover."

MARK 16:17-18

[Jesus said,] "But you will receive power when the Holy Spirit has come upon you, and you will be my witnesses in Jerusalem and in all Judea and Samaria, and to the end of the earth."

ACTS 1:8

God gave us a spirit not of fear but of power and love and self-control.

2 TIMOTHY 1:7

But our citizenship is in heaven, and from it we await a Savior, the Lord Jesus Christ, who will transform our lowly body to be like his glorious body, by the power that enables him even to subject all things to himself.

PHILIPPIANS 3:20-21

# ENCOURAGEMENT

Why are you cast down, O my soul,
   and why are you in turmoil within me?
Hope in God; for I shall again praise him,
   my salvation and my God.

PSALM 42:5-6

Cast your burden on the LORD,
   and he will sustain you;
he will never permit
   the righteous to be moved.

PSALM 55:22

When [the disciples] had preached the gospel to that city and had made many disciples, they returned to Lystra and to Iconium and to Antioch, strengthening the souls of the disciples, encouraging them to continue in the faith, and saying that through many tribulations we must enter the kingdom of God.

ACTS 14:21-22

[Jesus said,] "I have said these things to you, that in me you may have peace. In the world you will have tribulation. But take heart; I have overcome the world."

JOHN 16:33

Be steadfast, immovable, always abounding in the work of the Lord, knowing that in the Lord your labor is not in vain.

1 CORINTHIANS 15:58

A word fitly spoken
is like apples of gold in a setting of silver.

PROVERBS 25:11

What then shall we say to these things? . . . For I am sure that neither death nor life, nor angels nor rulers, nor things present nor things to come, nor powers, nor height nor depth, nor anything else in all creation, will be able to separate us from the love of God in Christ Jesus our Lord.

ROMANS 8:31, 38-39

Count it all joy, my brothers, when you meet trials of various kinds, for you know that the testing of your faith produces steadfastness. And let steadfastness have its full effect, that you may be perfect and complete, lacking in nothing.

JAMES 1:2-4

# ENDURANCE

And let us not grow weary of doing good, for in due season we will reap, if we do not give up.

GALATIANS 6:9

Seek the LORD and his strength;
    seek his presence continually!

1 CHRONICLES 16:11

Therefore, my beloved brothers, be steadfast, immovable, always abounding in the work of the Lord, knowing that in the Lord your labor is not in vain.

1 CORINTHIANS 15:58

Praying at all times in the Spirit. . . . To that end keep alert with all perseverance, making supplication for all the saints.

EPHESIANS 6:18

And I am sure of this, that he who began a good work in you will bring it to completion at the day of Jesus Christ.

PHILIPPIANS 1:6

Let us hold true to what we have attained.

PHILIPPIANS 3:16

If we endure, we will also reign with him.

2 TIMOTHY 2:12

Let us hold fast the confession of our hope without wavering, for he who promised is faithful.

HEBREWS 10:23

Therefore, since we are surrounded by so great a cloud of witnesses, let us also lay aside every weight, and sin which clings so closely, and let us run with endurance the race that is set before us, looking to Jesus, the founder and perfecter of our faith, who for the joy that was set before him endured the cross, despising the shame, and is seated at the right hand of the throne of God.

HEBREWS 12:1-13

Rejoice in hope, be patient in tribulation, be constant in prayer.

ROMANS 12:12

I have fought the good fight, I have finished the race, I have kept the faith.

2 TIMOTHY 4:7

# EQUALITY

There is neither Jew nor Greek, there is neither slave nor free, there is neither male nor female, for you are all one in Christ Jesus.

GALATIANS 3:28

"If I have rejected the cause of my manservant or
      my maidservant,
   when they brought a complaint against me,
what then shall I do when God rises up?
   When he makes inquiry, what shall I answer
      him?
Did not he who made me in the womb make him?
   And did not one fashion us in the womb?"

JOB 31:13-15

Then God said, "Let us make man in our image, after our likeness. And let them have dominion over the fish of the sea and over the birds of the heavens and over the livestock and over all the earth and over every creeping thing that creeps on the earth."
   So God created man in his own image,
   in the image of God he created him;
   male and female he created them.

GENESIS 1:26-27

# EXALTATION

God exalted [Jesus] at his right hand as Leader and
Savior, to give repentance to Israel and forgiveness
of sins.

ACTS 5:31

The pride of your heart has deceived you,
　you who live in the clefts of the rock,
　in your lofty dwelling,
who say in your heart,
　"Who will bring me down to the ground?"
Though you soar aloft like the eagle,
　though your nest is set among the stars,
　from there I will bring you down,
　declares the LORD.

OBADIAH 3-4

Let the one who boasts, boast in the Lord. For it is not
the one who commends himself who is approved,
but the one whom the Lord commends.

2 CORINTHIANS 10:17-18

For if anyone thinks he is something, when he is
nothing, he deceives himself.

GALATIANS 6:3

Let no one deceive you in any way. For that day will not come, unless the rebellion comes first, and the man of lawlessness is revealed, the son of destruction, who opposes and exalts himself against every so-called god or object of worship, so that he takes his seat in the temple of God, proclaiming himself to be God.

2 THESSALONIANS 2:3-4

God raised [Jesus] up, and of that we all are witnesses. Being therefore exalted at the right hand of God, and having received from the Father the promise of the Holy Spirit, he has poured out this that you yourselves are seeing and hearing.

ACTS 2:32-33

Therefore God has highly exalted [Christ Jesus] and bestowed on him the name that is above every name, so that at the name of Jesus every knee should bow, in heaven and on earth and under the earth, and every tongue confess that Jesus Christ is Lord, to the glory of God the Father.

PHILIPPIANS 2:9-11

# EXPECTANCY

Therefore, preparing your minds for action, and being sober-minded, set your hope fully on the grace that will be brought to you at the revelation of Jesus Christ.

1 PETER 1:13

For the creation was subjected to futility, not willingly, but because of him who subjected it, in hope that the creation itself will be set free from its bondage to decay and obtain the freedom of the glory of the children of God. For we know that the whole creation has been groaning together in the pains of childbirth until now. And not only the creation, but we ourselves, who have the firstfruits of the Spirit, groan inwardly as we wait eagerly for adoption as sons, the redemption of our bodies. For in this hope we were saved. Now hope that is seen is not hope. For who hopes for what he sees? But if we hope for what we do not see, we wait for it with patience.

ROMANS 8:20-25

Let us hold fast the confession of our hope without wavering, for he who promised is faithful.

HEBREWS 10:23

# EXULTATION

Let the heavens be glad, and let the earth rejoice,
    and let them say among the nations, "The LORD
        reigns!"
Let the sea roar, and all that fills it;
    let the field exult, and everything in it!

              1 CHRONICLES 16:31-32

I will be glad and exult in you;
    I will sing praise to your name, O Most High.

              PSALM 9:2

Let the righteous one rejoice in the LORD
    and take refuge in him!
Let all the upright in heart exult!

              PSALM 64:10

But the righteous shall be glad;
    they shall exult before God;
    they shall be jubilant with joy!

              PSALM 68:3

The LORD your God is in your midst,
    a mighty one who will save;
he will rejoice over you with gladness;
    he will quiet you by his love;
he will exult over you with loud singing.

              ZEPHANIAH 3:17

# FAITH

Now faith is the assurance of things hoped for, the conviction of things not seen.

HEBREWS 11:1

For God so loved the world, that he gave his only Son, that whoever believes in him should not perish but have eternal life.

JOHN 3:16

Trust in the LORD with all your heart,
    and do not lean on your own understanding.

PROVERBS 3:5

For [Christ's] sake I have suffered the loss of all things and count them as rubbish, in order that I may gain Christ and be found in him, not having a righteousness of my own that comes from the law, but that which comes through faith in Christ, the righteousness from God that depends on faith.

PHILIPPIANS 3:8-9

Jesus said to her, "I am the resurrection and the life. Whoever believes in me, though he die, yet shall he live, and everyone who lives and believes in me shall never die. Do you believe this?"

JOHN 11:25-26

Blessed is the man who trusts in the LORD,
    whose trust is the LORD.
He is like a tree planted by water,
    that sends out its roots by the stream,
and does not fear when heat comes,
    for its leaves remain green,
and is not anxious in the year of drought,
    for it does not cease to bear fruit.

JEREMIAH 17:7-8

[Jesus said,] "Truly, I say to you, if you have faith like a grain of mustard seed, you will say to this mountain, 'Move from here to there,' and it will move, and nothing will be impossible for you."

MATTHEW 17:20

And [Jesus] said to the woman, "Your faith has saved you; go in peace."

LUKE 7:50

The apostles said to the Lord, "Increase our faith!"

LUKE 17:5

While [Jesus] was still speaking, someone from the ruler's house came and said, "Your daughter is dead; do not trouble the Teacher any more." But Jesus on hearing this answered him, "Do not fear; only believe, and she will be well."

LUKE 8:49-50

Therefore, since we have been justified by faith, we have peace with God through our Lord Jesus Christ.

ROMANS 5:1

For by grace you have been saved through faith. And this is not your own doing; it is the gift of God.

EPHESIANS 2:8

If any of you lacks wisdom, let him ask God, who gives generously to all without reproach, and it will be given him. But let him ask in faith, with no doubting, for the one who doubts is like a wave of the sea that is driven and tossed by the wind.

JAMES 1:5-6

What good is it, my brothers, if someone says he has faith but does not have works? Can that faith save him? . . . Show me your faith apart from your works, and I will show you my faith by my works.

JAMES 2:14, 18

Trust in the LORD, and do good;
    dwell in the land and befriend faithfulness. . . .
Commit your way to the LORD;
    trust in him, and he will act.

PSALM 37:3, 5

Fight the good fight of the faith. Take hold of the eternal life to which you were called and about which you made the good confession in the presence of many witnesses.

1 TIMOTHY 6:12

# FELLOWSHIP WITH GOD

That which we have seen and heard we proclaim also to you, so that you too may have fellowship with us; and indeed our fellowship is with the Father and with his Son Jesus Christ.

1 JOHN 1:3

If we say we have fellowship with him while we walk in darkness, we lie and do not practice the truth.

1 JOHN 1:6

[Jesus said,] "No longer do I call you servants, for the servant does not know what his master is doing; but I have called you friends, for all that I have heard from my Father I have made known to you."

JOHN 15:15

Whoever says he abides in him ought to walk in the same way in which he walked.

1 JOHN 2:6

Jesus answered him, "If anyone loves me, he will keep my word, and my Father will love him, and we will come to him and make our home with him."

JOHN 14:23

I will walk among you and will be your God, and you shall be my people.

LEVITICUS 26:12

And I heard a loud voice from the throne saying, "Behold, the dwelling place of God is with man. He will dwell with them, and they will be his people, and God himself will be with them as their God. He will wipe away every tear from their eyes, and death shall be no more, neither shall there be mourning nor crying nor pain anymore, for the former things have passed away."

REVELATION 21:3-4

[Jesus said,] "For where two or three are gathered in my name, there am I among them."

MATTHEW 18:20

Whoever keeps [Christ's] commandments abides in him, and he in them. And by this we know that he abides in us, by the Spirit whom he has given us.

1 JOHN 3:24

But he who is joined to the Lord becomes one spirit with him.

1 CORINTHIANS 6:17

[Jesus said,] "For whoever does the will of my Father in heaven is my brother and sister and mother."

MATTHEW 12:50

# FELLOWSHIP WITH HUMANS

[Jesus prayed,] "A new commandment I give to you, that you love one another: just as I have loved you, you also are to love one another."

JOHN 13:34

Do two walk together,
  unless they have agreed to meet?

AMOS 3:3

[Jesus prayed,] "I do not ask for these only, but also for those who will believe in me through their word, that they may all be one, just as you, Father, are in me, and I in you, that they also may be in us, so that the world may believe that you have sent me."

JOHN 17:20-21

All these with one accord were devoting themselves to prayer, together with the women and Mary the mother of Jesus, and his brothers.

ACTS 1:14

And they devoted themselves to the apostles' teaching and fellowship, to the breaking of bread and the prayers.

ACTS 2:42

I appeal to you, brothers, by the name of our Lord Jesus Christ, that all of you agree and that there be no divisions among you, but that you be united in the same mind and the same judgment.

1 CORINTHIANS 1:10

So then, as we have opportunity, let us do good to everyone, and especially to those who are of the household of faith.

GALATIANS 6:10

And we urge you, brothers, admonish the idle, encourage the fainthearted, help the weak, be patient with them all.

1 THESSALONIANS 5:14

Therefore, confess your sins to one another and pray for one another, that you may be healed. The prayer of a righteous person has great power as it is working.

JAMES 5:16

Finally, all of you, have unity of mind, sympathy, brotherly love, a tender heart, and a humble mind. Do not repay evil for evil or reviling for reviling, but on the contrary, bless, for to this you were called, that you may obtain a blessing.

1 PETER 3:8-9

Beloved, let us love one another, for love is from God, and whoever loves has been born of God and knows God.

1 JOHN 4:7

# FILLING OF THE SPIRIT

"The Spirit of God has made me,
    and the breath of the Almighty gives me life."

JOB 33:4

See, I have called by name Bezalel the son of Uri,
son of Hur, of the tribe of Judah, and I have filled
him with the Spirit of God, with ability and intelli-
gence, with knowledge and all craftsmanship.

EXODUS 31:2-3

But as for me, I am filled with power,
    with the Spirit of the LORD,
    and with justice and might,
to declare to Jacob his transgression
    and to Israel his sin.

MICAH 3:8

"Do not be anxious how you are to speak or what you
are to say, for what you are to say will be given to
you in that hour. For it is not you who speak, but
the Spirit of your Father speaking through you."

MATTHEW 10:19-20

"But it is the spirit in man,
    the breath of the Almighty, that makes him
        understand."

JOB 32:8

[Jesus said,] "But you will receive power when the Holy Spirit has come upon you, and you will be my witnesses in Jerusalem and in all Judea and Samaria, and to the end of the earth."

ACTS 1:8

And suddenly there came from heaven a sound like a mighty rushing wind, and it filled the entire house where they were sitting. And divided tongues as of fire appeared to them and rested on each one of them. And they were all filled with the Holy Spirit and began to speak in other tongues as the Spirit gave them utterance.

ACTS 2:2-4

And the Spirit of the LORD shall rest upon him,
    the Spirit of wisdom and understanding,
    the Spirit of counsel and might,
    the Spirit of knowledge and the fear of the LORD.

ISAIAH 11:2

And when he had said this, he breathed on them and said to them, "Receive the Holy Spirit."

JOHN 20:22

By the Holy Spirit who dwells within us, guard the good deposit entrusted to you.

2 TIMOTHY 1:14

By this we know that we abide in him and he in us, because he has given us of his Spirit.

1 JOHN 4:13

[Jesus said,] "Nevertheless, I tell you the truth: it is to your advantage that I go away, for if I do not go away, the Helper will not come to you. But if I go, I will send him to you. . . . When the Spirit of truth comes, he will guide you into all the truth, for he will not speak on his own authority, but whatever he hears he will speak, and he will declare to you the things that are to come. He will glorify me, for he will take what is mine and declare it to you."

JOHN 16:7, 13-14

Then they laid their hands on them and they received the Holy Spirit.

ACTS 8:17

And the disciples were filled with joy and with the Holy Spirit.

ACTS 13:52

Now we have received not the spirit of the world, but the Spirit who is from God, that we might understand the things freely given us by God. And we impart this in words not taught by human wisdom but taught by the Spirit, interpreting spiritual truths to those who are spiritual.

1 CORINTHIANS 2:12-13

Do you not know that you are God's temple and that God's Spirit dwells in you?

1 CORINTHIANS 3:16

# Forgiving Others

"For if you forgive others their trespasses, your heavenly Father will also forgive you, but if you do not forgive others their trespasses, neither will your Father forgive your trespasses."

MATTHEW 6:14-15

"And whenever you stand praying, forgive, if you have anything against anyone, so that your Father also who is in heaven may forgive you your trespasses."

MARK 11:25

Be kind to one another, tenderhearted, forgiving one another, as God in Christ forgave you.

EPHESIANS 4:32

"Judge not, and you will not be judged; condemn not, and you will not be condemned; forgive, and you will be forgiven; give, and it will be given to you. Good measure, pressed down, shaken together, running over, will be put into your lap. For with the measure you use it will be measured back to you."

LUKE 6:37-38

Good sense makes one slow to anger,
and it is his glory to overlook an offense.

PROVERBS 19:11

Put on then, as God's chosen ones, holy and beloved, compassion, kindness, humility, meekness, and patience, bearing with one another and, if one has a complaint against another, forgiving each other; as the Lord has forgiven you, so you also must forgive.

COLOSSIANS 3:12-13

[Jesus prayed,] "And forgive us our sins,
    for we ourselves forgive everyone who is
        indebted to us."

LUKE 11:4

Beloved, never avenge yourselves, but leave it to the wrath of God, for it is written, "Vengeance is mine, I will repay, says the Lord."

ROMANS 12:19

# FRIENDSHIP

A friend loves at all times,
   and a brother is born for adversity.

PROVERBS 17:17

But Ruth said, "Do not urge me to leave you or to
return from following you. For where you go I will go,
and where you lodge I will lodge. Your people shall be
my people, and your God my God. Where you die I
will die, and there will I be buried. May the LORD do
so to me and more also if anything but death parts
me from you."

RUTH 1:16-17

Faithful are the wounds of a friend;
   profuse are the kisses of an enemy.

PROVERBS 27:6

Now as they went on their way, Jesus entered a vil-
lage. And a woman named Martha welcomed him
into her house. And she had a sister called Mary, who
sat at the Lord's feet and listened to his teaching.

LUKE 10:38-39

He who withholds kindness from a friend
   forsakes the fear of the Almighty.

JOB 6:14

Now Jesus loved Martha and her sister and Lazarus. So, when he heard that Lazarus was ill, he stayed two days longer in the place where he was. . . . After saying these things, [Jesus] said to them, "Our friend Lazarus has fallen asleep, but I go to awaken him."

JOHN 11:5-6, 11

A man of many companions may come to ruin,
but there is a friend who sticks closer than a brother.

PROVERBS 18:24

Two are better than one, because they have a good reward for their toil. For if they fall, one will lift up his fellow. But woe to him who is alone when he falls and has not another to lift him up! Again, if two lie together, they keep warm, but how can one keep warm alone? And though a man might prevail against one who is alone, two will withstand him—a threefold cord is not quickly broken.

ECCLESIASTES 4:9-12

Do two walk together,
unless they have agreed to meet?

AMOS 3:3

# GENTLENESS

[Jesus said,] "Take my yoke upon you, and learn from me, for I am gentle and lowly in heart, and you will find rest for your souls."

MATTHEW 11:29

If anyone is caught in any transgression, you who are spiritual should restore him in a spirit of gentleness. Keep watch on yourself, lest you too be tempted.

GALATIANS 6:1

Remind [believers] to be submissive to rulers and authorities, to be obedient, to be ready for every good work, to speak evil of no one, to avoid quarreling, to be gentle, and to show perfect courtesy toward all people.

TITUS 3:1-2

He will tend his flock like a shepherd;
    he will gather the lambs in his arms;
he will carry them in his bosom,
    and gently lead those that are with young.

ISAIAH 40:11

The fruit of the Spirit is love, joy, peace, patience, kindness, goodness, faithfulness, gentleness, and self-control.

GALATIANS 5:22-23

# GODLINESS

Train yourself for godliness; for while bodily training is of some value, godliness is of value in every way, as it holds promise for the present life and also for the life to come.

1 TIMOTHY 4:7-8

For this very reason, make every effort to supplement your faith with virtue, and virtue with knowledge, and knowledge with self-control, and self-control with steadfastness, and steadfastness with godliness.

2 PETER 1:5-6

Now there is great gain in godliness with contentment, for we brought nothing into the world, and we cannot take anything out of the world. But if we have food and clothing, with these we will be content.

1 TIMOTHY 6:6-8

If a widow has children or grandchildren, let them first learn to show godliness to their own household and to make some return to their parents, for this is pleasing in the sight of God.

1 TIMOTHY 5:4

But as for you, O man of God, flee these things. Pursue righteousness, godliness, faith, love, steadfastness, gentleness.

1 TIMOTHY 6:11

For the grace of God has appeared, bringing salvation for all people, training us to renounce ungodliness and worldly passions, and to live self-controlled, upright, and godly lives in the present age.

TITUS 2:11-12

Women should adorn themselves in respectable apparel, with modesty and self-control, not with braided hair and gold or pearls or costly attire, but with what is proper for women who profess godliness—with good works.

1 TIMOTHY 2:9-10

# Good Deeds

In the same way, let your light shine before others, so that they may see your good works and give glory to your Father who is in heaven.

MATTHEW 5:16

[Jesus said,] "By this my Father is glorified, that you bear much fruit and so prove to be my disciples."

JOHN 15:8

Now there was in Joppa a disciple named Tabitha, which, translated, means Dorcas. She was full of good works and acts of charity.

ACTS 9:36

Women should adorn themselves in respectable apparel, with modesty and self-control, not with braided hair and gold or pearls or costly attire, but with what is proper for women who profess godliness—with good works.

1 TIMOTHY 2:9-10

So also faith by itself, if it does not have works, is dead.

JAMES 2:17

And let us consider how to stir up one another to love and good works.

HEBREWS 10:24

Let a widow be enrolled if she is not less than sixty years of age, having been the wife of one husband, and having a reputation for good works: if she has brought up children, has shown hospitality, has washed the feet of the saints, has cared for the afflicted, and has devoted herself to every good work.

1 TIMOTHY 5:8-10

As for the rich in this present age, charge them not to . . . set their hopes on the uncertainty of riches, but on God. . . . They are to do good, to be rich in good works, to be generous and ready to share, thus storing up treasure for themselves as a good foundation for the future, so that they may take hold of that which is truly life.

1 TIMOTHY 6:17-19

# GUARANTEES

And it is God who establishes us with you in Christ, and has anointed us, and who has also put his seal on us and given us his Spirit in our hearts as a guarantee.

2 CORINTHIANS 1:21-22

That is why it depends on faith, in order that the promise may rest on grace and be guaranteed to all his offspring.

ROMANS 4:16

Blessed be the LORD who has given rest to his people Israel, according to all that he promised. Not one word has failed of all his good promise.

1 KINGS 8:56

Let us hold fast the confession of our hope without wavering, for he who promised is faithful.

HEBREWS 10:23

For all the promises of God find their Yes in [Christ]. That is why it is through him that we utter our Amen to God for his glory.

2 CORINTHIANS 1:20

# HEART

You shall love the LORD your God with all your heart
and with all your soul and with all your might.

DEUTERONOMY 6:5

Keep your heart with all vigilance,
   for from it flow the springs of life.

PROVERBS 4:23

This day the LORD your God commands you to do
these statutes and rules. You shall therefore be care-
ful to do them with all your heart and with all your
soul.

DEUTERONOMY 26:16

Every way of a man is right in his own eyes,
   but the LORD weighs the heart.

PROVERBS 21:2

Create in me a clean heart, O God,
   and renew a right spirit within me.

PSALM 51:10

And I will give you a new heart, and a new spirit I
will put within you. And I will remove the heart of
stone from your flesh and give you a heart of flesh.

EZEKIEL 36:26

The plans of the heart belong to man,
    but the answer of the tongue is from the LORD.

PROVERBS 16:1

Let your heart therefore be wholly true to the LORD
our God, walking in his statutes and keeping his
commandments, as at this day.

1 KINGS 8:61

Wait for the LORD;
    be strong, and let your heart take courage;
    wait for the LORD!

PSALM 27:14

Draw near to God, and he will draw near to you.
Cleanse your hands, you sinners, and purify your
hearts, you double-minded.

JAMES 4:8

For with the heart one believes and is justified, and
with the mouth one confesses and is saved.

ROMANS 10:10

Trust in the LORD with all your heart,
    and do not lean on your own understanding.

PROVERBS 3:5

Having purified your souls by your obedience to the
truth for a sincere brotherly love, love one another
earnestly from a pure heart.

1 PETER 1:22

# HEROINES OF THE FAITH

Now Deborah, a prophetess, the wife of Lappidoth, was judging Israel at that time. She used to sit under the palm of Deborah between Ramah and Bethel in the hill country of Ephraim, and the people of Israel came up to her for judgment.

JUDGES 4:4-5

But Ruth said, "Do not urge me to leave you or to return from following you. For where you go I will go, and where you lodge I will lodge. Your people shall be my people, and your God my God. Where you die I will die, and there will I be buried. May the LORD do so to me and more also if anything but death parts me from you." And when Naomi saw that she was determined to go with her, she said no more.

RUTH 1:16-18

But Hannah had no children. . . . She was deeply distressed and prayed to the LORD and wept bitterly. And she vowed a vow and said, "O LORD of hosts, if you will indeed look on the affliction of your servant and remember me and not forget your servant, but will give to your servant a son, then I will give him to the LORD all the days of his life."

1 SAMUEL 1:2, 10-11

Then Esther told them to reply to Mordecai, "Go, gather all the Jews to be found in Susa, and hold a fast on my behalf, and do not eat or drink for three days, night or day. I and my young women will also fast as you do. Then I will go to the king, though it is against the law, and if I perish, I perish."

ESTHER 4:15-16

In the sixth month the angel Gabriel was sent from God to a city of Galilee named Nazareth, to a virgin betrothed to a man whose name was Joseph, of the house of David. And the virgin's name was Mary.

LUKE 1:26-27

In the days of Herod, king of Judea, there was a priest named Zechariah, of the division of Abijah. And he had a wife from the daughters of Aaron, and her name was Elizabeth. And they were both righteous before God, walking blamelessly in all the commandments and statutes of the Lord.

LUKE 1:5-6

And while he was at Bethany in the house of Simon the leper, as he was reclining at table, a woman came with an alabaster flask of ointment of pure nard, very costly, and she broke the flask and poured it over his head.

MARK 14:3

When the Sabbath was past, Mary Magdalene and Mary the mother of James and Salome bought spices, so that they might go and anoint him.

MARK 16:1

Now there was in Joppa a disciple named Tabitha, which, translated, means Dorcas. She was full of good works and acts of charity.

ACTS 9:36

One who heard us was a woman named Lydia, from the city of Thyatira, a seller of purple goods, who was a worshiper of God. The Lord opened her heart to pay attention to what was said by Paul.

ACTS 16:14

I commend to you our sister Phoebe, a servant of the church at Cenchreae, that you may welcome her in the Lord in a way worthy of the saints, and help her in whatever she may need from you, for she has been a patron of many and of myself as well.

ROMANS 16:1-2

I am reminded of your sincere faith, a faith that dwelt first in your grandmother Lois and your mother Eunice and now, I am sure, dwells in you as well.

2 TIMOTHY 1:5

# IMAGE

Then God said, "Let us make man in our image, after our likeness. And let them have dominion over the fish of the sea and over the birds of the heavens and over the livestock and over all the earth and over every creeping thing that creeps on the earth."

So God created man in his own image,
in the image of God he created him;
male and female he created them.

GENESIS 1:26-27

For those whom he foreknew he also predestined to be conformed to the image of his Son, in order that he might be the firstborn among many brothers.

ROMANS 8:29

And we all, with unveiled face, beholding the glory of the Lord, are being transformed into the same image from one degree of glory to another. For this comes from the Lord who is the Spirit.

2 CORINTHIANS 3:18

Beloved, we are God's children now, and what we will be has not yet appeared; but we know that when he appears we shall be like him, because we shall see him as he is.

1 JOHN 3:2

[Christ] is the image of the invisible God, the first-born of all creation.

COLOSSIANS 1:15

Do you not know that you are God's temple and that God's Spirit dwells in you?

1 CORINTHIANS 3:16

Do not let your adorning be external—the braiding of hair, the wearing of gold, or the putting on of clothing—but let your adorning be the hidden person of the heart with the imperishable beauty of a gentle and quiet spirit, which in God's sight is very precious.

1 PETER 3:3-4

Therefore, if anyone is in Christ, he is a new creation. The old has passed away; behold, the new has come.

2 CORINTHIANS 5:17

# Inheritance

The righteous shall inherit the land
    and dwell upon it forever.

PSALM 37:29

And now I commend you to God and to the word of
his grace, which is able to build you up and to give
you the inheritance among all those who are sanctified.

ACTS 20:32

An inheritance gained hastily in the beginning
    will not be blessed in the end.

PROVERBS 20:21

The Spirit himself bears witness with our spirit that
we are children of God, and if children, then heirs—
heirs of God and fellow heirs with Christ, provided
we suffer with him in order that we may also be glorified with him.

ROMANS 8:16-17

In [Christ] we have obtained an inheritance, having
been predestined according to the purpose of him
who works all things according to the counsel of his
will.

EPHESIANS 1:11

# JEALOUSY

You shall worship no other god, for the LORD, whose name is Jealous, is a jealous God.

EXODUS 34:13-14

I am the LORD; that is my name;
   my glory I give to no other,
   nor my praise to carved idols.

ISAIAH 42:8

Jealousy makes a man furious,
   and he will not spare when he takes revenge.

PROVERBS 6:34

Set me as a seal upon your heart,
   as a seal upon your arm,
for love is strong as death,
   jealousy is fierce as the grave.
Its flashes are flashes of fire,
   the very flame of the LORD.

SONG 8:6

Let us walk properly as in the daytime, not in orgies and drunkenness, not in sexual immorality and sensuality, not in quarreling and jealousy.

ROMANS 13:13

"Therefore wait for me," declares the LORD,
  "for the day when I rise up to seize the prey.
For my decision is to gather nations,
  to assemble kingdoms,
to pour out upon them my indignation,
  all my burning anger;
for in the fire of my jealousy
  all the earth shall be consumed."

ZEPHANIAH 3:8

You shall not covet your neighbor's house; you shall not covet your neighbor's wife, or his male servant, or his female servant, or his ox, or his donkey, or anything that is your neighbor's.

EXODUS 20:17

For you are still of the flesh. For while there is jealousy and strife among you, are you not of the flesh and behaving only in a human way?

1 CORINTHIANS 3:3

But if you have bitter jealousy and selfish ambition in your hearts, do not boast and be false to the truth. . . . For where jealousy and selfish ambition exist, there will be disorder and every vile practice.

JAMES 3:14, 16

# JESUS

There shall come forth a shoot from the stump of
        Jesse,
    and a branch from his roots shall bear fruit.
And the Spirit of the LORD shall rest upon him,
    the Spirit of wisdom and understanding,
    the Spirit of counsel and might,
    the Spirit of knowledge and the fear of the LORD.

ISAIAH 11:1-2

And the Word became flesh and dwelt among us, and
we have seen his glory, glory as of the only Son from
the Father, full of grace and truth.

JOHN 1:14

"She will bear a son, and you shall call his name
Jesus, for he will save his people from their sins."

MATTHEW 1:21

For he grew up before him like a young plant,
    and like a root out of dry ground;
he had no form or majesty that we should look at
        him,
    and no beauty that we should desire him.
He was despised and rejected by men;
    a man of sorrows, and acquainted with grief.

ISAIAH 53:2-3

And Jesus increased in wisdom and in stature and in favor with God and man.

LUKE 2:52

The stone that the builders rejected
    has become the cornerstone.

PSALM 118:22

[Jesus said,] "For as the lightning flashes and lights up the sky from one side to the other, so will the Son of Man be in his day. But first he must suffer many things and be rejected by this generation."

LUKE 17:24-25

He was oppressed, and he was afflicted,
    yet he opened not his mouth;
like a lamb that is led to the slaughter,
    and like a sheep that before its shearers is silent,
    so he opened not his mouth.

ISAIAH 53:7

"Jesus of Nazareth, a man attested to you by God with mighty works and wonders and signs that God did through him in your midst, as you yourselves know—this Jesus, delivered up according to the definite plan and foreknowledge of God, you crucified and killed by the hands of lawless men. God raised him up, loosing the pangs of death, because it was not possible for him to be held by it."

ACTS 2:22-24

# JEWELRY

In that day the Lord will take away the finery of the anklets, the headbands, and the crescents; the pendants, the bracelets, and the scarves; the headdresses, the armlets, the sashes, the perfume boxes, and the amulets; the signet rings and nose rings.

ISAIAH 3:18-21

There is gold and abundance of costly stones,
    but the lips of knowledge are a precious jewel.

PROVERBS 20:15

And we have brought the LORD's offering, what each man found, articles of gold, armlets and bracelets, signet rings, earrings, and beads, to make atonement for ourselves before the LORD.

NUMBERS 31:50

Do not let your adorning be external—the braiding of hair, the wearing of gold, or the putting on of clothing—but let your adorning be the hidden person of the heart with the imperishable beauty of a gentle and quiet spirit, which in God's sight is very precious. For this is how the holy women who hoped in God used to adorn themselves, by submitting to their husbands.

1 PETER 3:3-5

# Joy

Then he said to them, "Go your way. Eat the fat and drink sweet wine and send portions to anyone who has nothing ready, for this day is holy to our Lord. And do not be grieved, for the joy of the Lord is your strength."

NEHEMIAH 8:10

But let all who take refuge in you rejoice;
    let them ever sing for joy,
and spread your protection over them,
    that those who love your name may exult in you.

PSALM 5:11

[Jesus said,] "So also you have sorrow now, but I will see you again and your hearts will rejoice, and no one will take your joy from you."

JOHN 16:22

You make known to me the path of life;
    in your presence there is fullness of joy;
    at your right hand are pleasures forevermore.

PSALM 16:11

But the fruit of the Spirit is love, joy, peace, patience, kindness, goodness, faithfulness . . .

GALATIANS 5:22

[Jesus said,] "Until now you have asked nothing in my name. Ask, and you will receive, that your joy may be full."

JOHN 16:24

For you shall go out in joy
    and be led forth in peace;
the mountains and the hills before you
    shall break forth into singing,
        and all the trees of the field shall clap their hands.

ISAIAH 55:12

For the kingdom of God is not a matter of eating and drinking but of righteousness and peace and joy in the Holy Spirit.

ROMANS 14:17

Then shall the young women rejoice in the dance,
    and the young men and the old shall be merry.
I will turn their mourning into joy;
    I will comfort them, and give them gladness for
        sorrow.

JEREMIAH 31:13

Rejoice in hope, be patient in tribulation, be constant in prayer.

ROMANS 12:12

Count it all joy, my brothers, when you meet trials of various kinds, for you know that the testing of your faith produces steadfastness.

JAMES 1:2-3

# KINDNESS

You shall treat the stranger who sojourns with you as the native among you, and you shall love him as yourself, for you were strangers in the land of Egypt: I am the LORD your God.

LEVITICUS 19:34

Love is patient and kind.

1 CORINTHIANS 13:4

Be kind to one another, tenderhearted, forgiving one another, as God in Christ forgave you.

EPHESIANS 4:32

Finally, all of you, have unity of mind, sympathy, brotherly love, a tender heart, and a humble mind. Do not repay evil for evil or reviling for reviling, but on the contrary, bless, for to this you were called, that you may obtain a blessing.

1 PETER 3:8-9

But if anyone has the world's goods and sees his brother in need, yet closes his heart against him, how does God's love abide in him? Little children, let us not love in word or talk but in deed and in truth.

1 JOHN 3:17-18

# KINGDOM METAPHOR— BRIDE

I will greatly rejoice in the LORD;
  my soul shall exult in my God,
for he has clothed me with the garments of salvation;
  he has covered me with the robe of righteousness,
as a bridegroom decks himself like a priest with a
      beautiful headdress,
  and as a bride adorns herself with her jewels.

ISAIAH 61.10

Husbands, love your wives, as Christ loved the church and gave himself up for her, that he might sanctify her, having cleansed her by the washing of water with the word, so that he might present the church to himself in splendor, without spot or wrinkle or any such thing, that she might be holy and without blemish. . . . This mystery is profound, and I am saying that it refers to Christ and the church.

EPHESIANS 5:25-27, 32

Let us rejoice and exult
  and give him the glory,
for the marriage of the Lamb has come,
  and his Bride has made herself ready.

REVELATION 19:7

# KINGDOM METAPHOR—
# DAUGHTER

Rejoice greatly, O daughter of Zion!
Shout aloud, O daughter of Jerusalem!
behold, your king is coming to you;
righteous and having salvation is he,
humble and mounted on a donkey,
on a colt, the foal of a donkey.

ZECHARIAH 9:9

Be gracious to me, O LORD!
See my affliction from those who hate me,
O you who lift me up from the gates of death,
that I may recount all your praises,
that in the gates of the daughter of Zion
I may rejoice in your salvation.

PSALM 9:13-14

"Why do you boast of your valleys,
O faithless daughter,
who trusted in her treasures, saying,
'Who will come against me?'"

JEREMIAH 49:4

# KINGDOM METAPHOR—
# MOTHER

As one whom his mother comforts,
    so I will comfort you;
    you shall be comforted in Jerusalem.

ISAIAH 66:13

"Behold, everyone who uses proverbs will use this proverb about you: 'Like mother, like daughter.' You are the daughter of your mother, who loathed her husband and her children; and you are the sister of your sisters, who loathed their husbands and their children."

EZEKIEL 16:44-45

But now hear, O Jacob my servant,
    Israel whom I have chosen!
Thus says the LORD who made you,
    who formed you from the womb and will help
        you:
Fear not, O Jacob my servant.

ISAIAH 44:1-2

But we were gentle among you, like a nursing mother taking care of her own children.

1 THESSALONIANS 2:7

Thus says the LORD: "Where is your mother's
      certificate of divorce,
  with which I sent her away? . . .
Behold, for your iniquities you were sold,
    and for your transgressions your mother was
      sent away."

ISAIAH 50:1

What was your mother? A lioness!
    Among lions she crouched;
in the midst of young lions
    she reared her cubs.

EZEKIEL 19:2

But I have calmed and quieted my soul,
    like a weaned child with its mother;
    like a weaned child is my soul within me.

PSALM 131:2

# KINGDOM METAPHOR— PREGNANCY

Writhe and groan, O daughter of Zion,
    like a woman in labor,
for now you shall go out from the city
    and dwell in the open country;
    you shall go to Babylon.
There you shall be rescued;
    there the LORD will redeem you
    from the hand of your enemies.

MICAH 4:10

. . . by the God of your father who will help you,
    by the Almighty who will bless you
    with blessings of heaven above,
blessings of the deep that crouches beneath,
    blessings of the breasts and of the womb.

GENESIS 49:25

"Or who shut in the sea with doors
    when it burst out from the womb . . . ?"

JOB 38:8

"From whose womb did the ice come forth,
    and who has given birth to the frost of heaven?"

JOB 38:29

Behold, the wicked man conceives evil
　　and is pregnant with mischief
　　and gives birth to lies.

PSALM 7:14

The wicked are estranged from the womb;
　　they go astray from birth, speaking lies.

PSALM 58:3

Like a pregnant woman
　　who writhes and cries out in her pangs
　　when she is near to giving birth,
so were we because of you, O LORD;
　　we were pregnant, we writhed,
　　but we have given birth to wind.
We have accomplished no deliverance in the earth,
　　and the inhabitants of the world have not fallen.

ISAIAH 26:17-18

For nation will rise against nation, and kingdom
against kingdom. There will be earthquakes in various places; there will be famines. These are but the
beginning of the birth pains.

MARK 13:8

# KNOWLEDGE

And out of the ground the LORD God made to spring up every tree that is pleasant to the sight and good for food. The tree of life was in the midst of the garden, and the tree of the knowledge of good and evil.

GENESIS 2:9

Then the LORD God said, "Behold, the man has become like one of us in knowing good and evil. Now, lest he reach out his hand and take also of the tree of life and eat, and live forever—" therefore the LORD God sent him out from the garden of Eden to work the ground from which he was taken.

GENESIS 3:22-23

The LORD by wisdom founded the earth;
    by understanding he established the heavens;
by his knowledge the deeps broke open,
    and the clouds drop down the dew.

PROVERBS 3:19-20

To one is given through the Spirit the utterance of wisdom, and to another the utterance of knowledge according to the same Spirit.

1 CORINTHIANS 12:8

A wise man is full of strength,
    and a man of knowledge enhances his might.

PROVERBS 24:5

My son, if you receive my words
    and treasure up my commandments with you,
making your ear attentive to wisdom
    and inclining your heart to understanding;
yes, if you call out for insight
    and raise your voice for understanding,
if you seek it like silver
    and search for it as for hidden treasures,
then you will understand the fear of the LORD
    and find the knowledge of God.

PROVERBS 2:1-5

An intelligent heart acquires knowledge,
    and the ear of the wise seeks knowledge.

PROVERBS 18:15

You will go before the Lord to prepare his ways,
    to give knowledge of salvation to his people
in the forgiveness of their sins.

LUKE 1:76-77

# LEADERSHIP

"But now go, lead the people to the place about which I have spoken to you; behold, my angel shall go before you."

EXODUS 32:34

[Jesus] also told them a parable: "Can a blind man lead a blind man? Will they not both fall into a pit?"

LUKE 6:39

Shepherd the flock of God that is among you, exercising oversight, not under compulsion, but willingly, as God would have you; not for shameful gain, but eagerly; not domineering over those in your charge, but being examples to the flock.

1 PETER 5:2-3

For false christs and false prophets will arise and perform great signs and wonders, so as to lead astray, if possible, even the elect.

MATTHEW 24:24

Let no one despise you for your youth, but set the believers an example in speech, in conduct, in love, in faith, in purity.

1 TIMOTHY 4:12

# LIGHT

And God said, "Let there be light," and there was light.

GENESIS 1:3

Light is sown for the righteous,
and joy for the upright in heart.

PSALM 97:11

Your word is a lamp to my feet
and a light to my path.

PSALM 119:105

"You are the light of the world. A city set on a hill cannot be hidden. . . . let your light shine before others, so that they may see your good works and give glory to your Father who is in heaven."

MATTHEW 5:14, 16

Again Jesus spoke to them, saying, "I am the light of the world. Whoever follows me will not walk in darkness, but will have the light of life."

JOHN 8:12

Whoever loves his brother abides in the light, and in him there is no cause for stumbling.

1 JOHN 2:10

The LORD is my light and my salvation;
    whom shall I fear?
The LORD is the stronghold of my life;
    of whom shall I be afraid?

PSALM 27:1

The unfolding of your words gives light;
    it imparts understanding to the simple.

PSALM 119:130

Commit your way to the LORD;
    trust in him, and he will act.
He will bring forth your righteousness as the light,
    and your justice as the noonday.

PSALM 37:5-6

In [the Word] was life, and the life was the light of
men. The light shines in the darkness, and the darkness has not overcome it.

JOHN 1:4-5

# LOVING GOD

You shall love the LORD your God with all your heart
and with all your soul and with all your might.

DEUTERONOMY 6:5

You shall therefore love the LORD your God and keep
his charge, his statutes, his rules, and his commandments always.

DEUTERONOMY 11:1

The LORD preserves all who love him,
 but all the wicked he will destroy.

PSALM 145:20

And he said to him, "You shall love the Lord your
God with all your heart and with all your soul
and with all your mind. This is the great and first
commandment."

MATTHEW 22:37-38

May the Lord direct your hearts to the love of God
and to the steadfastness of Christ.

2 THESSALONIANS 3:5

We love because he first loved us.

1 JOHN 4:19

If anyone says, "I love God," and hates his brother, he is a liar; for he who does not love his brother whom he has seen cannot love God whom he has not seen.

1 JOHN 4:20

I love the LORD, because he has heard
my voice and my pleas for mercy.

PSALM 116:1

For this is the love of God, that we keep his commandments. And his commandments are not burdensome.

1 JOHN 5:3

But if anyone loves God, he is known by God.

1 CORINTHIANS 8:3

# LOVING OTHERS

Beloved, let us love one another, for love is from God, and whoever loves has been born of God and knows God.

1 JOHN 4:7

And this commandment we have from him: whoever loves God must also love his brother.

1 JOHN 4:21

[Jesus said,] "A new commandment I give to you, that you love one another: just as I have loved you, you also are to love one another."

JOHN 13:34

Now concerning brotherly love you have no need for anyone to write to you, for you yourselves have been taught by God to love one another.

1 THESSALONIANS 4:9

But the fruit of the Spirit is love, joy, peace, patience, kindness, goodness, faithfulness . . .

GALATIANS 5:22

[Jesus said,] "But I say to you, Love your enemies and pray for those who persecute you."

MATTHEW 5:44

Having purified your souls by your obedience to the truth for a sincere brotherly love, love one another earnestly from a pure heart.

1 PETER 1:22

Love one another with brotherly affection. Outdo one another in showing honor.

ROMANS 12:10

Husbands, love your wives, as Christ loved the church and gave himself up for her.

EPHESIANS 5:25

And so train the young women to love their husbands and children.

TITUS 2:4

You shall treat the stranger who sojourns with you as the native among you, and you shall love him as yourself, for you were strangers in the land of Egypt: I am the LORD your God.

LEVITICUS 19:34

For you were called to freedom, brothers. Only do not use your freedom as an opportunity for the flesh, but through love serve one another.

GALATIANS 5:13

[Jesus said,] "By this all people will know that you are my disciples, if you have love for one another."

JOHN 13:35

# LOYALTY

A man of many companions may come to ruin,
but there is a friend who sticks closer than a
brother.

PROVERBS 18:24

My son, fear the LORD and the king,
and do not join with those who do otherwise.

PROVERBS 24:21

When he came and saw the grace of God, he was
glad, and he exhorted them all to remain faithful to
the Lord with steadfast purpose.

ACTS 11:23

Many a man proclaims his own steadfast love,
but a faithful man who can find?

PROVERBS 20:6

A friend loves at all times,
and a brother is born for adversity.

PROVERBS 17:17

Two are better than one, because they have a good
reward for their toil. For if they fall, one will lift up his
fellow.

ECCLESIASTES 4:9-10

# MARRIAGE

Then the man said,
"This at last is bone of my bones
   and flesh of my flesh;
she shall be called Woman,
   because she was taken out of Man."
   Therefore a man shall leave his father and his
      mother and hold fast to his wife, and they
      shall become one flesh.

GENESIS 2:23-24

The husband should give to his wife her conjugal
rights, and likewise the wife to her husband. For the
wife does not have authority over her own body, but the
husband does. Likewise the husband does not have
authority over his own body, but the wife does. Do
not deprive one another, except perhaps by agreement
for a limited time, that you may devote yourselves to
prayer; but then come together again, so that Satan may
not tempt you because of your lack of self-control.

1 CORINTHIANS 7:3-5

But because of the temptation to sexual immorality,
each man should have his own wife and each woman
her own husband.

1 CORINTHIANS 7:2

To the married I give this charge (not I, but the Lord):
the wife should not separate from her husband (but
if she does, she should remain unmarried or else be
reconciled to her husband), and the husband should
not divorce his wife.

1 CORINTHIANS 7:10-11

Wives, submit to your own husbands, as to the Lord.
For the husband is the head of the wife even as Christ
is the head of the church, his body, and is himself
its Savior. Now as the church submits to Christ, so
also wives should submit in everything to their husbands.

EPHESIANS 5:22-24

Let marriage be held in honor among all, and let the
marriage bed be undefiled, for God will judge the sex-
ually immoral and adulterous.

HEBREWS 13:4

[Jesus] answered, "Have you not read that he who
created them from the beginning made them male
and female, and said, 'Therefore a man shall leave
his father and his mother and hold fast to his wife,
and they shall become one flesh'? So they are no
longer two but one flesh. What therefore God has
joined together, let not man separate."

MATTHEW 19:4-6

# MIRACLES

[Jesus said,] "But the testimony that I have is greater than that of John. For the works that the Father has given me to accomplish, the very works that I am doing, bear witness about me that the Father has sent me."

JOHN 5:36

[Nicodemus] came to Jesus by night and said to him, "Rabbi, we know that you are a teacher come from God, for no one can do these signs that you do unless God is with him."

JOHN 3.2

Now Jesus did many other signs in the presence of the disciples, which are not written in this book; but these are written so that you may believe that Jesus is the Christ, the Son of God, and that by believing you may have life in his name.

JOHN 20:30-31

"But for this purpose I have raised you up, to show you my power, so that my name may be proclaimed in all the earth."

EXODUS 9:16

# Modesty

Women should adorn themselves in respectable apparel, with modesty and self-control, not with braided hair and gold or pearls or costly attire.

1 TIMOTHY 2:9

The Lord said:
Because the daughters of Zion are haughty
 and walk with outstretched necks,
 glancing wantonly with their eyes,
mincing along as they go,
 tinkling with their feet,
therefore the Lord will strike with a scab
 the heads of the daughters of Zion,
 and the Lord will lay bare their secret parts.

ISAIAH 3:16-17

Do not let your adorning be external—the braiding of hair, the wearing of gold, or the putting on of clothing—but let your adorning be the hidden person of the heart with the imperishable beauty of a gentle and quiet spirit, which in God's sight is very precious.

1 PETER 3:3-4

# MOTHERHOOD

Honor your father and your mother, as the LORD your God commanded you, that your days may be long, and that it may go well with you in the land that the LORD your God is giving you.

DEUTERONOMY 5:16

A wise son makes a glad father,
    but a foolish son is a sorrow to his mother.

PROVERBS 10:1

I am reminded of your sincere faith, a faith that dwelt first in your grandmother Lois and your mother Eunice and now, I am sure, dwells in you as well.

2 TIMOTHY 1:5

Then the woman whose son was alive said to the king, because her heart yearned for her son, "Oh, my lord, give her the living child, and by no means put him to death." But the other said, "He shall be neither mine nor yours; divide him." Then the king answered and said, "Give the living child to the first woman, and by no means put him to death; she is his mother."

1 KINGS 3:26-27

Praise the LORD! Praise, O servants of the LORD,
     praise the name of the LORD! . . .
He gives the barren woman a home,
     making her the joyous mother of children.
Praise the LORD!

PSALM 113:1, 9

Stretching out his hand toward his disciples, [Jesus]
said, "Here are my mother and my brothers! For whoever does the will of my Father in heaven is my
brother and sister and mother."

MATTHEW 12:49-50

And [Jesus] went down with them and came to
Nazareth and was submissive to them. And his
mother treasured up all these things in her heart.

LUKE 2:51

As one whom his mother comforts,
     so I will comfort you;
     you shall be comforted in Jerusalem.

ISAIAH 66:13

When Jesus saw his mother and the disciple whom
he loved standing nearby, he said to his mother,
"Woman, behold, your son!" Then he said to the
disciple, "Behold, your mother!" And from that hour
the disciple took her to his own home.

JOHN 19:26-27

# PARDON OF SIN

I, I am he
   who blots out your transgressions for my own
        sake,
   and I will not remember your sins.

ISAIAH 43:25

Come now, let us reason together, says the LORD:
though your sins are like scarlet,
   they shall be as white as snow;
though they are red like crimson,
   they shall become like wool.

ISAIAH 1:18

In those days and in that time, declares the LORD,
iniquity shall be sought in Israel, and there shall be
none. And sin in Judah, and none shall be found,
for I will pardon those whom I leave as a remnant.

JEREMIAH 50:20

Let the wicked forsake his way,
   and the unrighteous man his thoughts;
let him return to the LORD, that he may have
        compassion on him,
   and to our God, for he will abundantly pardon.

ISAIAH 55:7

# PATIENCE

[God] will render to each one according to his works: to those who by patience in well-doing seek for glory and honor and immortality, he will give eternal life.

ROMANS 2:6-7

Rejoice in hope, be patient in tribulation, be constant in prayer.

ROMANS 12:12

Put on then, as God's chosen ones, holy and beloved, compassion, kindness, humility, meekness, and patience, bearing with one another and, if one has a complaint against another, forgiving each other; as the Lord has forgiven you, so you also must forgive.

COLOSSIANS 3:12-13

Be patient, therefore, brothers, until the coming of the Lord. See how the farmer waits for the precious fruit of the earth, being patient about it, until it receives the early and the late rains. You also, be patient. Establish your hearts, for the coming of the Lord is at hand.

JAMES 5:7-8

# PERFECTION

"You therefore must be perfect, as your heavenly Father is perfect."

MATTHEW 5:48

Jesus said to him, "If you would be perfect, go, sell what you possess and give to the poor, and you will have treasure in heaven; and come, follow me."

MATTHEW 19:21

For we all stumble in many ways, and if anyone does not stumble in what he says, he is a perfect man, able also to bridle his whole body.

JAMES 3:2

Not that I have already obtained this or am already perfect, but I press on to make it my own, because Christ Jesus has made me his own.

PHILIPPIANS 3:12

And let steadfastness have its full effect, that you may be perfect and complete, lacking in nothing.

JAMES 1:4

# PLEASANTNESS

The lines have fallen for me in pleasant places;
 indeed, I have a beautiful inheritance.

PSALM 16:6

Behold, how good and pleasant it is
 when brothers dwell in unity!

PSALM 133:1

Praise the LORD! For it is good to sing praises to our
 God;
 for it is pleasant, and a song of praise is fitting.

PSALM 147:1

For the moment all discipline seems painful rather
than pleasant, but later it yields the peaceful fruit of
righteousness to those who have been trained by it.

HEBREWS 12:11

For wisdom will come into your heart,
 and knowledge will be pleasant to your soul.

PROVERBS 2:10

How beautiful and pleasant you are,
 O loved one, with all your delights!

SONG 7:6

# PLEASURE

Whoever loves pleasure will be a poor man;
    he who loves wine and oil will not be rich.

PROVERBS 21:17

I said in my heart, "Come now, I will test you with
pleasure; enjoy yourself." But behold, this also was
vanity. I said of laughter, "It is mad," and of pleasure, "What use is it?"

ECCLESIASTES 2:1-2

"And as for what fell among the thorns, they are those
who hear, but as they go on their way they are choked
by the cares and riches and pleasures of life, and their
fruit does not mature."

LUKE 8:14

You make known to me the path of life;
    in your presence there is fullness of joy;
    at your right hand are pleasures forevermore.

PSALM 16:11

# POWER OF GOD

But Jesus looked at them and said, "With man this is impossible, but with God all things are possible."

MATTHEW 19:26

Once God has spoken;
twice have I heard this:
that power belongs to God.

PSALM 62:11

The voice of the LORD is over the waters;
the God of glory thunders,
the LORD, over many waters. . . .
The voice of the LORD breaks the cedars;
the LORD breaks the cedars of Lebanon.

PSALM 29:3, 5

For his invisible attributes, namely, his eternal power and divine nature, have been clearly perceived, ever since the creation of the world, in the things that have been made. So they are without excuse.

ROMANS 1:20

. . . what is the immeasurable greatness of his power toward us who believe, according to the working of his great might.

EPHESIANS 1:19

When I look at your heavens, the work of your
      fingers,
  the moon and the stars, which you have set in
      place,
what is man that you are mindful of him,
  and the son of man that you care for him?

PSALM 8:3-4

The LORD your God is in your midst,
  a mighty one who will save;
he will rejoice over you with gladness;
  he will quiet you by his love;
he will exult over you with loud singing.

ZEPHANIAH 3:17

Now to him who is able to do far more abundantly
than all that we ask or think, according to the power
at work within us, to him be glory in the church and
in Christ Jesus throughout all generations, forever
and ever. Amen.

EPHESIANS 3:20-21

# PRAYER

[Jesus said,] "Ask, and it will be given to you; seek, and you will find; knock, and it will be opened to you. For everyone who asks receives, and the one who seeks finds, and to the one who knocks it will be opened."

MATTHEW 7:7-8

And there was a prophetess, Anna, the daughter of Phanuel, of the tribe of Asher. She was advanced in years, having lived with her husband seven years from when she was a virgin, and then as a widow until she was eighty-four. She did not depart from the temple, worshiping with fasting and prayer night and day.

LUKE 2:36-37

[Jesus said,] "Therefore I tell you, whatever you ask in prayer, believe that you have received it, and it will be yours."

MARK 11:24

If my people who are called by my name humble themselves, and pray and seek my face and turn from their wicked ways, then I will hear from heaven and will forgive their sin and heal their land.

2 CHRONICLES 7:14

You have said, "Seek my face."
My heart says to you,
"Your face, LORD, do I seek."

PSALM 27:8

The LORD is near to all who call on him,
to all who call on him in truth.

PSALM 145:18

But Hannah had no children. . . . She was deeply
distressed and prayed to the LORD and wept bitterly.
And she vowed a vow and said, "O LORD of hosts, if
you will indeed look on the affliction of your servant
and remember me and not forget your servant, but
will give to your servant a son, then I will give him
to the LORD all the days of his life."

1 SAMUEL 1:2, 10-11

And [Hannah] said, "Oh, my lord! As you live, my lord,
I am the woman who was standing here in your presence, praying to the LORD. For this child I prayed, and
the LORD has granted me my petition that I made to
him."

1 SAMUEL 1:26-27

Seek the LORD while he may be found;
call upon him while he is near;

ISAIAH 55:6

Do not be anxious about anything, but in everything
by prayer and supplication with thanksgiving let your
requests be made known to God.

PHILIPPIANS 4:6

[Jesus said,] "Pray then like this:

'Our Father in heaven,
     hallowed be your name.
  Your kingdom come,
  your will be done,
       on earth as it is in heaven.
  Give us this day our daily bread,
  and forgive us our debts,
       as we also have forgiven our debtors.
  And lead us not into temptation,
       but deliver us from evil.'"

MATTHEW 6:9-13

Likewise the Spirit helps us in our weakness. For we do not know what to pray for as we ought, but the Spirit himself intercedes for us with groanings too deep for words.

ROMANS 8:26

Pray without ceasing.

1 THESSALONIANS 5:17

# PRECIOUSNESS

How precious is your steadfast love, O God!
　　The children of mankind take refuge in the
　　　　shadow of your wings.

PSALM 36:7

Precious in the sight of the LORD
　　is the death of his saints.

PSALM 116:15

How precious to me are your thoughts, O God!
　　How vast is the sum of them!

PSALM 139:17

Do not let your adorning be external—the braiding of
hair, the wearing of gold, or the putting on of clothing—but let your adorning be the hidden person of
the heart with the imperishable beauty of a gentle and
quiet spirit, which in God's sight is very precious.

1 PETER 3:3-4

But I do not account my life of any value nor as precious to myself, if only I may finish my course and the
ministry that I received from the Lord Jesus, to testify to the gospel of the grace of God.

ACTS 20:24

Blessed is the one who finds wisdom,
and the one who gets understanding,
for the gain from her is better than gain from silver
and her profit better than gold.
She is more precious than jewels,
and nothing you desire can compare with her.

PROVERBS 3:13-15

An excellent wife who can find?
She is far more precious than jewels.

PROVERBS 31:10

A good name is better than precious ointment,
and the day of death than the day of birth.

ECCLESIASTES 7:1

For it stands in Scripture:

"Behold, I am laying in Zion a stone,
a cornerstone chosen and precious,
and whoever believes in him will not be put to
shame."

1 PETER 2:6

# PROMISES

"Repent and be baptized every one of you in the name of Jesus Christ for the forgiveness of your sins, and you will receive the gift of the Holy Spirit. For the promise is for you and for your children and for all who are far off, everyone whom the Lord our God calls to himself."

ACTS 2:38-39

"Your offspring shall be like the dust of the earth, and you shall spread abroad to the west and to the east and to the north and to the south, and in you and your offspring shall all the families of the earth be blessed."

GENESIS 28:14

Now the promises were made to Abraham and to his offspring. It does not say, "And to offsprings," referring to many, but referring to one, "And to your offspring," who is Christ.

GALATIANS 3:16

But as it is, Christ has obtained a ministry that is as much more excellent than the old as the covenant he mediates is better, since it is enacted on better promises.

HEBREWS 8:6

Let us hold fast the confession of our hope without wavering, for he who promised is faithful.

HEBREWS 10:23

For all the promises of God find their Yes in [Christ]. That is why it is through him that we utter our Amen to God for his glory.

2 CORINTHIANS 1:20

Is the law then contrary to the promises of God? Certainly not! For if a law had been given that could give life, then righteousness would indeed be by the law.

GALATIANS 3:21

Blessed is the man who remains steadfast under trial, for when he has stood the test he will receive the crown of life, which God has promised to those who love him.

JAMES 1:12

And this is the promise that he made to us—eternal life.

1 JOHN 2:25

# Protection

For God alone my soul waits in silence;
    from him comes my salvation.
He only is my rock and my salvation,
    my fortress; I shall not be greatly shaken.

PSALM 62:1-2

The LORD is a stronghold for the oppressed,
    a stronghold in times of trouble.

PSALM 9:9

For he will hide me in his shelter
    in the day of trouble;
he will conceal me under the cover of his tent;
    he will lift me high upon a rock.

PSALM 27:5

You . . . by God's power are being guarded through faith for a salvation ready to be revealed in the last time.

1 PETER 1:4-5

[Jesus said,] "Because you have kept my word about patient endurance, I will keep you from the hour of trial that is coming on the whole world, to try those who dwell on the earth."

REVELATION 3:10

In peace I will both lie down and sleep;
for you alone, O LORD, make me dwell in safety.

PSALM 4:8

But the Lord is faithful. He will establish you and
guard you against the evil one.

2 THESSALONIANS 3:3

God is our refuge and strength,
a very present help in trouble.

PSALM 46:1

Be strong and courageous. Do not fear or be in dread
of them, for it is the LORD your God who goes with
you. He will not leave you or forsake you.

DEUTERONOMY 31:6

# PURIFICATION

Purge me with hyssop, and I shall be clean;
  wash me, and I shall be whiter than snow.

PSALM 51:7

Let us draw near with a true heart in full assurance
of faith, with our hearts sprinkled clean from an evil
conscience and our bodies washed with pure water.

HEBREWS 10:22

Indeed, under the law almost everything is purified
with blood, and without the shedding of blood there
is no forgiveness of sins.

HEBREWS 9:22

How much more will the blood of Christ, who
through the eternal Spirit offered himself without
blemish to God, purify our conscience from dead
works to serve the living God.

HEBREWS 9:14

Draw near to God, and he will draw near to you.
Cleanse your hands, you sinners, and purify your
hearts, you double-minded.

JAMES 4:8

# PURITY

So flee youthful passions and pursue righteousness, faith, love, and peace, along with those who call on the Lord from a pure heart.

2 TIMOTHY 2:22

Finally, brothers, whatever is true, whatever is honorable, whatever is just, whatever is pure, whatever is lovely, whatever is commendable, if there is any excellence, if there is anything worthy of praise, think about these things.

PHILIPPIANS 4:8

The aim of our charge is love that issues from a pure heart and a good conscience and a sincere faith.

1 TIMOTHY 1:5

Treat younger men like brothers, older women like mothers, younger women like sisters, in all purity.

1 TIMOTHY 5:1-2

Let us draw near with a true heart in full assurance of faith, with our hearts sprinkled clean from an evil conscience and our bodies washed with pure water.

HEBREWS 10:22

# PURPOSES OF GOD

For we are his workmanship, created in Christ Jesus for good works, which God prepared beforehand, that we should walk in them.

EPHESIANS 2:10

It is God who works in you, both to will and to work for his good pleasure.

PHILIPPIANS 2:13

[Jesus] said, "To you it has been given to know the secrets of the kingdom of God, but for others they are in parables, so that seeing they may not see, and hearing they may not understand."

LUKE 8:10

[Jesus said,] "And this is the will of him who sent me, that I should lose nothing of all that he has given me, but raise it up on the last day."

JOHN 6:39

For God did not send his Son into the world to condemn the world, but in order that the world might be saved through him.

JOHN 3:17

God our Savior . . . desires all people to be saved and to come to the knowledge of the truth.

1 TIMOTHY 2:3-4

# REFRESHMENT

Trust in the LORD with all your heart,
    and do not lean on your own understanding.
In all your ways acknowledge him,
    and he will make straight your paths.
Be not wise in your own eyes;
    fear the LORD, and turn away from evil.
It will be healing to your flesh
    and refreshment to your bones.

PROVERBS 3:5-8

Yes, brother, I want some benefit from you in the Lord. Refresh my heart in Christ.

PHILEMON 20

In your steadfast love give me life,
    that I may keep the testimonies of your mouth.

PSALM 119:88

You who seek God, let your hearts revive.

PSALM 69:32

After two days he will revive us;
    on the third day he will raise us up,
    that we may live before him.

HOSEA 6:2

# REJOICING

⟜❦⟝

Yet I will rejoice in the LORD;
  I will take joy in the God of my salvation.

HABAKKUK 3:18

[Jesus said,] "These things I have spoken to you, that my joy may be in you, and that your joy may be full."

JOHN 15:11

And the ransomed of the LORD shall return
  and come to Zion with singing;
everlasting joy shall be upon their heads;
  they shall obtain gladness and joy,
  and sorrow and sighing shall flee away.

ISAIAH 51:11

Though you have not seen him, you love him. Though you do not now see him, you believe in him and rejoice with joy that is inexpressible and filled with glory, obtaining the outcome of your faith, the salvation of your souls.

1 PETER 1:8-9

Rejoice in hope, be patient in tribulation, be constant in prayer.

ROMANS 12:12

And Hannah prayed and said,
"My heart exults in the LORD;
    my strength is exalted in the LORD.
My mouth derides my enemies,
    because I rejoice in your salvation."

1 SAMUEL 2:1

Let the heavens be glad, and let the earth rejoice,
    and let them say among the nations, "The LORD
        reigns!"

1 CHRONICLES 16:31

Then the people rejoiced because they had given willingly, for with a whole heart they had offered freely to the LORD.

1 CHRONICLES 29:9

The precepts of the LORD are right,
    rejoicing the heart;
the commandment of the LORD is pure,
    enlightening the eyes.

PSALM 19:8

Be glad in the LORD, and rejoice, O righteous,
and shout for joy, all you upright in heart!

PSALM 32:11

Rejoice with those who rejoice, weep with those who weep.

ROMANS 12:15

Rejoice in the Lord always; again I will say, Rejoice.

PHILIPPIANS 4:4

For it is written,

"Rejoice, O barren one who does not bear;
　　break forth and cry aloud, you who are not in
　　　　labor!
For the children of the desolate one will be more
　　than those of the one who has a husband."

GALATIANS 4:27

But rejoice insofar as you share Christ's sufferings,
that you may also rejoice and be glad when his glory
is revealed.

1 PETER 4:13

Let us rejoice and exult
　　and give him the glory,
for the marriage of the Lamb has come,
　　and his Bride has made herself ready.

REVELATION 19:7

# RESTORATION

Therefore thus says the LORD:
"If you return, I will restore you,
　　and you shall stand before me."

JEREMIAH 15:19

He restores my soul. He leads me in paths of righteousness for his name's sake.

PSALM 23:3

Restore to me the joy of your salvation,
　　and uphold me with a willing spirit.

PSALM 51:12

And the LORD restored the fortunes of Job, when he had prayed for his friends. And the LORD gave Job twice as much as he had before.

JOB 42:10

Brothers, if anyone is caught in any transgression, you who are spiritual should restore him in a spirit of gentleness. Keep watch on yourself, lest you too be tempted.

GALATIANS 6:1

Blessed is the one who considers the poor!
    In the day of trouble the LORD delivers him;
the LORD protects him and keeps him alive;
    he is called blessed in the land;
    you do not give him up to the will of his
            enemies.
The LORD sustains him on his sickbed;
    in his illness you restore him to full health.

PSALM 41:1-3

Finally, brothers, rejoice. Aim for restoration, comfort one another, agree with one another, live in peace; and the God of love and peace will be with you.

2 CORINTHIANS 13:11

Restore us, O God;
    let your face shine, that we may be saved!

PSALM 80:3

And after you have suffered a little while, the God of all grace, who has called you to his eternal glory in Christ, will himself restore, confirm, strengthen, and establish you.

1 PETER 5:10

# RIGHTEOUSNESS OF GOD

The LORD is righteous in all his ways
and kind in all his works.

PSALM 145:17

Steadfast love and faithfulness meet;
righteousness and peace kiss each other.

PSALM 85:10

For all have sinned and fall short of the glory of God,
and are justified by his grace as a gift, through the
redemption that is in Christ Jesus, whom God put
forward as a propitiation by his blood, to be received
by faith. This was to show God's righteousness.

ROMANS 3:23-25

The LORD has made known his salvation;
he has revealed his righteousness in the sight of
the nations.

PSALM 98:2

For I am not ashamed of the gospel, for it is the power
of God for salvation to everyone who believes, to the
Jew first and also to the Greek. For in it the righteousness of God is revealed from faith for faith, as it
is written, "The righteous shall live by faith."

ROMANS 1:16-17

# ROMANTIC LOVE

So Jacob served seven years for Rachel, and they seemed to him but a few days because of the love he had for her.

GENESIS 29:20

Set me as a seal upon your heart,
    as a seal upon your arm,
for love is strong as death,
    jealousy is fierce as the grave.
Its flashes are flashes of fire,
    the very flame of the LORD.
Many waters cannot quench love,
    neither can floods drown it.
If a man offered for love
    all the wealth of his house,
    he would be utterly despised.

SONG 8:6-7

Love is patient and kind; love does not envy or boast; it is not arrogant or rude. It does not insist on its own way; it is not irritable or resentful; it does not rejoice at wrongdoing, but rejoices with the truth. Love bears all things, believes all things, hopes all things, endures all things.

1 CORINTHIANS 13:4-7

# SACRIFICE

The sacrifices of God are a broken spirit;
a broken and contrite heart, O God, you will not
despise.

PSALM 51:17

"Which commandment is the most important of all?"
Jesus answered, . . . "[To] love the Lord your God
with all your heart and with all your soul and with
all your mind and with all your strength. . . . and to
love one's neighbor as oneself, is much more than
all whole burnt offerings and sacrifices."

MARK 12:28-29

Walk in love, as Christ loved us and gave himself up
for us, a fragrant offering and sacrifice to God.

EPHESIANS 5:2

For it is impossible for the blood of bulls and goats
to take away sins.

HEBREWS 10:4

I appeal to you therefore, brothers, by the mercies of
God, to present your bodies as a living sacrifice, holy
and acceptable to God, which is your spiritual worship.

ROMANS 12:1

Consequently, when Christ came into the world, he said,

"Sacrifices and offerings you have not desired,
    but a body have you prepared for me;
in burnt offerings and sin offerings
    you have taken no pleasure."

HEBREWS 10:5-6

Truly no man can ransom another,
    or give to God the price of his life,
for the ransom of their life is costly
    and can never suffice.

PSALM 49:7-8

But whatever gain I had, I counted as loss for the sake of Christ. Indeed, I count everything as loss because of the surpassing worth of knowing Christ Jesus my Lord. For his sake I have suffered the loss of all things and count them as rubbish, in order that I may gain Christ.

PHILIPPIANS 3:7-8

Do not neglect to do good and to share what you have, for such sacrifices are pleasing to God.

HEBREWS 13:16

# SAINTS

As for the saints in the land, they are the excellent
        ones,
   in whom is all my delight.

PSALM 16:3

To all those in Rome who are loved by God and called
to be saints:
   Grace to you and peace from God our Father
and the Lord Jesus Christ.

ROMANS 1:7

And he who searches hearts knows what is the mind
of the Spirit, because the Spirit intercedes for the
saints according to the will of God.

ROMANS 8:27

For God is not so unjust as to overlook your work and
the love that you showed for his sake in serving the
saints, as you still do.

HEBREWS 6:10

So then you are no longer strangers and aliens, but
you are fellow citizens with the saints and members
of the household of God.

EPHESIANS 2:19

Oh, fear the LORD, you his saints,
for those who fear him have no lack!

PSALM 34:9

To the church of God that is in Corinth, to those
sanctified in Christ Jesus, called to be saints together
with all those who in every place call upon the name
of our Lord Jesus Christ, both their Lord and ours.

1 CORINTHIANS 1:2

Precious in the sight of the LORD
is the death of his saints.

PSALM 116:15

And he gave the apostles, the prophets, the evangel-
ists, the pastors and teachers, to equip the saints for
the work of ministry, for building up the body of
Christ.

EPHESIANS 4:11-12

# SALVATION

———⟡———

For by grace you have been saved through faith. And this is not your own doing; it is the gift of God.

EPHESIANS 2:8

For the wages of sin is death, but the free gift of God is eternal life in Christ Jesus our Lord.

ROMANS 6:23

Because, if you confess with your mouth that Jesus is Lord and believe in your heart that God raised him from the dead, you will be saved.

ROMANS 10:9

Salvation belongs to the LORD;
    your blessing be on your people!

PSALM 3:8

For God has not destined us for wrath, but to obtain salvation through our Lord Jesus Christ.

1 THESSALONIANS 5:9

Let your steadfast love come to me, O LORD,
    your salvation according to your promise.

PSALM 119:41

This Jesus is the stone that was rejected by you, the builders, which has become the cornerstone. And there is salvation in no one else, for there is no other name under heaven given among men by which we must be saved.

ACTS 4:11-12

For God so loved the world, that he gave his only Son, that whoever believes in him should not perish but have eternal life. For God did not send his Son into the world to condemn the world, but in order that the world might be saved through him.

JOHN 3:16-17

For God has not destined us for wrath, but to obtain salvation through our Lord Jesus Christ.

1 THESSALONIANS 5:9

Restore to me the joy of your salvation,
and uphold me with a willing spirit.

PSALM 51:12

# SINCERITY

"But the hour is coming, and is now here, when the true worshipers will worship the Father in spirit and truth, for the Father is seeking such people to worship him."

JOHN 4:23

For our boast is this: the testimony of our conscience that we behaved in the world with simplicity and godly sincerity, not by earthly wisdom but by the grace of God, and supremely so toward you.

2 CORINTHIANS 1:12

Now therefore fear the LORD and serve him in sincerity and in faithfulness. Put away the gods that your fathers served beyond the River and in Egypt, and serve the LORD.

JOSHUA 24:14

Blessed is the man against whom the LORD counts
         no iniquity,
     and in whose spirit there is no deceit.

PSALM 32:2

Show yourself in all respects to be a model of good works, and in your teaching show integrity, dignity.

TITUS 2:7

# SINGLENESS

I wish that all were as I myself am. But each has his own gift from God, one of one kind and one of another. To the unmarried and the widows I say that it is good for them to remain single as I am. But if they cannot exercise self-control, they should marry. For it is better to marry than to be aflame with passion.

1 CORINTHIANS 7:7 9

Now concerning the betrothed, I have no command from the Lord, but I give my judgment as one who by the Lord's mercy is trustworthy. I think that in view of the present distress it is good for a person to remain as he is. Are you bound to a wife? Do not seek to be free. Are you free from a wife? Do not seek a wife.

1 CORINTHIANS 7:25-27

The unmarried or betrothed woman is anxious about the things of the Lord, how to be holy in body and spirit. But the married woman is anxious about worldly things, how to please her husband.

1 CORINTHIANS 7:35

# Steadfastness

So then, brothers, stand firm and hold to the traditions that you were taught by us, either by our spoken word or by our letter.

2 THESSALONIANS 2:15

But let him ask in faith, with no doubting, for the one who doubts is like a wave of the sea that is driven and tossed by the wind.

JAMES 1:6

Therefore, my brothers, whom I love and long for, my joy and crown, stand firm thus in the Lord, my beloved.

PHILIPPIANS 4:1

He only is my rock and my salvation,
my fortress; I shall not be greatly shaken.

PSALM 62:2

When he came and saw the grace of God, he was glad, and he exhorted them all to remain faithful to the Lord with steadfast purpose.

ACTS 11:23

Test everything; hold fast what is good.

1 THESSALONIANS 5:21

Be steadfast, immovable, always abounding in the work of the Lord, knowing that in the Lord your labor is not in vain.

1 CORINTHIANS 15:58

Let us hold fast the confession of our hope without wavering, for he who promised is faithful.

HEBREWS 10:23

I have set the LORD always before me;
    because he is at my right hand, I shall not be
        shaken.

PSALM 16:8

Resist [the devil], firm in your faith, knowing that the same kinds of suffering are being experienced by your brotherhood throughout the world.

1 PETER 5:9

For freedom Christ has set us free; stand firm therefore, and do not submit again to a yoke of slavery.

GALATIANS 5:1

Now to him who is able to keep you from stumbling and to present you blameless before the presence of his glory with great joy, to the only God, our Savior, through Jesus Christ our Lord, be glory, majesty, dominion, and authority, before all time and now and forever. Amen.

JUDE 24-25

# SUPPLICATION

Do not be anxious about anything, but in everything by prayer and supplication with thanksgiving let your requests be made known to God.

PHILIPPIANS 4:6

First of all, then, I urge that supplications, prayers, intercessions, and thanksgivings be made for all people.

1 TIMOTHY 2:1

Give ear to my prayer, O God,
    and hide not yourself from my plea for mercy!

PSALM 55:1

Therefore, confess your sins to one another and pray for one another, that you may be healed. The prayer of a righteous person has great power as it is working.

JAMES 5:16

For the eyes of the Lord are on the righteous,
    and his ears are open to their prayer.
But the face of the Lord is against those who do evil.

1 PETER 3:12

# SYMPATHY

[Jesus said,] "For I was hungry and you gave me food, I was thirsty and you gave me drink, I was a stranger and you welcomed me, I was naked and you clothed me, I was sick and you visited me, I was in prison and you came to me.' . . . And the King will answer them, 'Truly, I say to you, as you did it to one of the least of these my brothers, you did it to me.'"

MATTHEW 25:35-36, 40

So if there is any encouragement in Christ, any comfort from love, any participation in the Spirit, any affection and sympathy, complete my joy by being of the same mind, having the same love, being in full accord and of one mind.

PHILIPPIANS 2:1-2

Religion that is pure and undefiled before God, the Father, is this: to visit orphans and widows in their affliction, and to keep oneself unstained from the world.

JAMES 1:27

[Jesus asked,] "Which of these three, do you think, proved to be a neighbor to the man who fell among the robbers?" He said, "The one who showed him mercy." And Jesus said to him, "You go, and do likewise."

LUKE 10:36-37

# TEACHING

Teach me to do your will,
    for you are my God!
Let your good Spirit lead me
    on level ground!

PSALM 143:10

Preach the word; be ready in season and out of season; reprove, rebuke, and exhort, with complete patience and teaching.

2 TIMOTHY 4:2

How can a young man keep his way pure?
    By guarding it according to your word.
With my whole heart I seek you;
    let me not wander from your commandments!
I have stored up your word in my heart,
    that I might not sin against you.
Blessed are you, O LORD;
    teach me your statutes!

PSALM 119:9-12

All Scripture is breathed out by God and profitable for teaching, for reproof, for correction, and for training in righteousness.

2 TIMOTHY 3:16

The fear of the LORD is the beginning of knowledge;
    fools despise wisdom and instruction.
Hear, my son, your father's instruction,
    and forsake not your mother's teaching,
for they are a graceful garland for your head
    and pendants for your neck.

PROVERBS 1:7-9

Apply your heart to instruction
    and your ear to words of knowledge.

PROVERBS 23:12

Buy truth, and do not sell it;
    buy wisdom, instruction, and understanding.

PROVERBS 23:23

Hear, O Israel: The LORD our God, the LORD is one.
You shall love the LORD your God with all your heart
and with all your soul and with all your might. And
these words that I command you today shall be on
your heart. You shall teach them diligently to your
children, and shall talk of them when you sit in your
house, and when you walk by the way, and when
you lie down, and when you rise.

DEUTERONOMY 6:4-7

Train up a child in the way he should go;
    even when he is old he will not depart from it.

PROVERBS 22:6

# TENDERNESS

He will tend his flock like a shepherd;
    he will gather the lambs in his arms;
he will carry them in his bosom,
    and gently lead those that are with young.

ISAIAH 40:11

Be kind to one another, tenderhearted, forgiving one
another, as God in Christ forgave you.

EPHESIANS 4:32

How can I give you up, O Ephraim?
    How can I hand you over, O Israel?
How can I make you like Admah?
    How can I treat you like Zeboiim?
My heart recoils within me;
    my compassion grows warm and tender.

HOSEA 11:8

When [Jesus] saw the crowds, he had compassion for
them, because they were harassed and helpless, like
sheep without a shepherd.

MATTHEW 9:36

Jesus wept.

JOHN 11:35

# TESTIMONY

Bind up the testimony; seal the teaching among my disciples.

ISAIAH 8:16

To the teaching and to the testimony! If they will not speak according to this word, it is because they have no dawn.

ISAIAH 8:20

[Jesus said,] "So everyone who acknowledges me before men, I also will acknowledge before my Father who is in heaven."

MATTHEW 10:32

So the woman left her water jar and went away into town and said to the people, "Come, see a man who told me all that I ever did. Can this be the Christ?" They went out of the town and were coming to him. . . . Many Samaritans from that town believed in him because of the woman's testimony, "He told me all that I ever did."

JOHN 4:28-30, 39

[Jesus said,] "And you also will bear witness, because you have been with me from the beginning."

JOHN 15:27

[Jesus said,] "But you will receive power when the Holy Spirit has come upon you, and you will be my witnesses in Jerusalem and in all Judea and Samaria, and to the end of the earth."

ACTS 1:8

If you confess with your mouth that Jesus is Lord and believe in your heart that God raised him from the dead, you will be saved.

ROMANS 10:9

I give thanks to my God always for you because of the grace of God that was given you in Christ Jesus, that in every way you were enriched in him in all speech and all knowledge.

1 CORINTHIANS 1:4-5

Therefore do not be ashamed of the testimony about our Lord, nor of me his prisoner, but share in suffering for the gospel by the power of God.

2 TIMOTHY 1:8

In your hearts regard Christ the Lord as holy, always being prepared to make a defense to anyone who asks you for a reason for the hope that is in you.

1 PETER 3:15

# THANKFULNESS

And whatever you do, in word or deed, do everything in the name of the Lord Jesus, giving thanks to God the Father through him.

COLOSSIANS 3:17

Give thanks in all circumstances; for this is the will of God in Christ Jesus for you.

1 THESSALONIANS 5:18

Give thanks to the LORD, for he is good, for his steadfast love endures forever.

PSALM 136:1

Thanks be to God, who gives us the victory through our Lord Jesus Christ.

1 CORINTHIANS 15:57

Do not be anxious about anything, but in everything by prayer and supplication with thanksgiving let your requests be made known to God.

PHILIPPIANS 4:6

Let us come into his presence with thanksgiving;
let us make a joyful noise to him with songs of
praise!

PSALM 95:2

# VIRTUE

For this very reason, make every effort to supplement your faith with virtue, and virtue with knowledge.

2 PETER 1:5

An excellent wife who can find?
    She is far more precious than jewels.

PROVERBS 31:10

Charm is deceitful, and beauty is vain,
    but a woman who fears the LORD is to be praised.

PROVERBS 31:30

Blessed is the man who walks not in the counsel of
        the wicked,
nor stands in the way of sinners,
    nor sits in the seat of scoffers;
but his delight is in the law of the LORD,
    and on his law he meditates day and night.
He is like a tree
    planted by streams of water
that yields its fruit in its season,
    and its leaf does not wither.
In all that he does, he prospers.

PSALM 1:1-3

# VOCATION

The gifts and the calling of God are irrevocable.

ROMANS 11:29

To this end we always pray for you, that our God may make you worthy of his calling and may fulfill every resolve for good and every work of faith by his power.

2 THESSALONIANS 1:11

You are the light of the world. A city set on a hill cannot be hidden. Nor do people light a lamp and put it under a basket, but on a stand, and it gives light to all in the house. In the same way, let your light shine before others, so that they may see your good works and give glory to your Father who is in heaven.

MATTHEW 5:14-16

For we are his workmanship, created in Christ Jesus for good works, which God prepared beforehand, that we should walk in them.

EPHESIANS 2:10

It is God who works in you, both to will and to work for his good pleasure.

PHILIPPIANS 2:13

# WEALTH

Better is the little that the righteous has
    than the abundance of many wicked.

PSALM 37:16

"Do not lay up for yourselves treasures on earth,
where moth and rust destroy and where thieves break
in and steal, but lay up for yourselves treasures in
heaven, where neither moth nor rust destroys and
where thieves do not break in and steal."

MATTHEW 6:19-20

But if anyone has the world's goods and sees his
brother in need, yet closes his heart against him, how
does God's love abide in him?

1 JOHN 3:17

Do not toil to acquire wealth;
    be discerning enough to desist.
When your eyes light on it, it is gone,
    for suddenly it sprouts wings,
      flying like an eagle toward heaven.

PROVERBS 23:4-5

Jesus said to him, "If you would be perfect, go, sell
what you possess and give to the poor, and you will
have treasure in heaven; and come, follow me."

MATTHEW 19:21

# WISDOM

The fear of the LORD is the beginning of knowledge;
fools despise wisdom and instruction.

PROVERBS 1:7

If any of you lacks wisdom, let him ask God, who
gives generously to all without reproach, and it will
be given him.

JAMES 1:5

Who is wise and understanding among you? By his
good conduct let him show his works in the meekness of wisdom.

JAMES 3:13

Oh, the depth of the riches and wisdom and knowledge of God! How unsearchable are his judgments
and how inscrutable his ways!

ROMANS 11:33

The wisdom of this world is folly with God.

1 CORINTHIANS 3:19

[Jesus said,] "Everyone then who hears these words
of mine and does them will be like a wise man who
built his house on the rock."

MATTHEW 7:24

"I said, 'Let days speak,
   and many years teach wisdom.'
But it is the spirit in man,
   the breath of the Almighty, that makes him
         understand."

JOB 32:7-8

No eye has seen, nor ear heard,
   nor the heart of man imagined,
what God has prepared for those who love him.

1 CORINTHIANS 2:9

Let no one deceive himself. If anyone among you
thinks that he is wise in this age, let him become a
fool that he may become wise.

1 CORINTHIANS 3:18

Look carefully then how you walk, not as unwise
but as wise, making the best use of the time, because
the days are evil.

EPHESIANS 5:15-16

# WORD OF GOD

For the word of God is living and active, sharper than any two-edged sword, piercing to the division of soul and of spirit, of joints and of marrow, and discerning the thoughts and intentions of the heart.

HEBREWS 4:12

All Scripture is breathed out by God and profitable for teaching, for reproof, for correction, and for training in righteousness.

2 TIMOTHY 3:16

The law of the Lord is perfect,
    reviving the soul;
the testimony of the Lord is sure,
    making wise the simple.

PSALM 19:7

You shall therefore lay up these words of mine in your heart and in your soul, and you shall bind them as a sign on your hand, and they shall be as frontlets between your eyes. You shall teach them to your children, talking of them when you are sitting in your house, and when you are walking by the way, and when you lie down, and when you rise.

DEUTERONOMY 11:18-19

Blessed is the man who walks not in the counsel of
      the wicked,
nor stands in the way of sinners,
    nor sits in the seat of scoffers;
but his delight is in the law of the LORD,
    and on his law he meditates day and night.

PSALM 1:1-2

The words of the LORD are pure words,
    like silver refined in a furnace on the ground,
    purified seven times.

PSALM 12:6

By the word of the LORD the heavens were made,
    and by the breath of his mouth all their host.

PSALM 33:6

But [Jesus] answered, "It is written,

'Man shall not live by bread alone,
    but by every word that comes from the mouth
      of God.'"

MATTHEW 4:4

So Jesus said . . . , "If you abide in my word, you are
truly my disciples, and you will know the truth, and
the truth will set you free."

JOHN 8:31-32

# WORSHIP

You shall worship no other god, for the LORD, whose name is Jealous, is a jealous God.

EXODUS 34:14

All the ends of the earth shall remember
    and turn to the LORD,
and all the families of the nations
    shall worship before you.

PSALM 22:27

And he sent them to Bethlehem, saying, "Go and search diligently for the child, and when you have found him, bring me word, that I too may come and worship him."

MATTHEW 2:8

But the hour is coming, and is now here, when the true worshipers will worship the Father in spirit and truth, for the Father is seeking such people to worship him.

JOHN 4:23

Then Jesus said to him, "Be gone, Satan! For it is written,

'You shall worship the Lord your God
    and him only shall you serve.'"

MATTHEW 4:10

Ascribe to the LORD the glory due his name;
 bring an offering, and come into his courts!
Worship the LORD in the splendor of holiness;
 tremble before him, all the earth!

PSALM 96:8-9

I will pray with my spirit, but I will pray with my mind also; I will sing praise with my spirit, but I will sing with my mind also.

1 CORINTHIANS 14:15

Blessed are those who dwell in your house,
 ever singing your praise!

PSALM 84:4

Therefore let us be grateful for receiving a kingdom that cannot be shaken, and thus let us offer to God acceptable worship, with reverence and awe.

HEBREWS 12:28

I appeal to you therefore, brothers, by the mercies of God, to present your bodies as a living sacrifice, holy and acceptable to God, which is your spiritual worship. Do not be conformed to this world, but be transformed by the renewal of your mind, that by testing you may discern what is the will of God, what is good and acceptable and perfect.

ROMANS 12:1-2

# WORTH

Indeed, I count everything as loss because of the surpassing worth of knowing Christ Jesus my Lord. For his sake I have suffered the loss of all things and count them as rubbish, in order that I may gain Christ

PHILIPPIANS 3:8

"Are not two sparrows sold for a penny? And not one of them will fall to the ground apart from your Father. But even the hairs of your head are all numbered. Fear not, therefore; you are of more value than many sparrows."

MATTHEW 10:29-31

"But I do not account my life of any value nor as precious to myself, if only I may finish my course and the ministry that I received from the Lord Jesus, to testify to the gospel of the grace of God."

ACTS 20:24

While bodily training is of some value, godliness is of value in every way, as it holds promise for the present life and also for the life to come.

1 TIMOTHY 4:8

# Youth

Remember not the sins of my youth or my
      transgressions;
   according to your steadfast love remember me,
   for the sake of your goodness, O Lord!

                            PSALM 25:7

For you, O Lord, are my hope,
   my trust, O Lord, from my youth.

                            PSALM 71:5

Bless the Lord, O my soul,
   and forget not all his benefits,
who forgives all your iniquity,
   who heals all your diseases,
who redeems your life from the pit,
   who crowns you with steadfast love and mercy,
who satisfies you with good
   so that your youth is renewed like the eagle's.

                      PSALM 103:2-5

Let no one despise you for your youth, but set the
believers an example in speech, in conduct, in love,
in faith, in purity.

                      1 TIMOTHY 4:12